IN THEIR
OWN WORDS

A History of
the American Negro

1916-1966

EDITED BY MILTON MELTZER

THOMAS Y. CROWELL COMPANY
NEW YORK

I wish to thank the *Journal of Negro History* for permission to reprint the letters on pages 3-5; Harper & Row for permission to use the passage on pages 8-14 from *Uncle Tom's Children* by Richard Wright, copyright 1937 by Richard Wright, and the excerpt on pages 176-184 from *Stride Toward Freedom* by Martin Luther King, Jr., copyright © 1958 by Martin Luther King, Jr.; Paul R. Reynolds, Inc., for permission to use the passage on pages 16-22 from *12 Million Black Voices* by Richard Wright, copyright 1941 by Richard Wright; the National Association for the Advancement of Colored People for permission to use excerpts from *The Crisis* on pages 25-27, 30-35, 52-54, 64-67; *The Nation* for permission to use the excerpts on pages 57-61, 70-73, and 97-100; Howard Zinn for supplying the documents on pages 188-190; the National Urban League for permission to use excerpts from *Opportunity* on pages 85-86, 89-94, 116-118, 132-136, and 152-155; the *New Republic* for permission to use the material on pages 140-146 and 158-161, copyright © 1940-1941, Harrison-Blaine of New Jersey, Inc.; the University of Chicago Press for permission to use the excerpt on pages 121-129 from *The Shadow of the Plantation* by Charles S. Johnson, copyright 1934 by University of Chicago Press; Alfred A. Knopf, Inc., for permission to use material on pages 168-172 from *South of Freedom* by Carl T. Rowan, copyright 1952 by Carl T. Rowan; Doubleday & Company, Inc., for permission to use the excerpt on pages 103-113 from *Scottsboro Boy* by Haywood Patterson and Earl Conrad, copyright 1950 by Earl Conrad; *Freedomways,* Langston Hughes, and Loften Mitchell for permission to use the material on pages 45-49, 75-82, and 146-149.

Thanks are due the following for permission to reproduce the illustrations on the pages indicated (all other illustrations are in the editor's collection): The Bettmann Archive, page 95; Brown Brothers, page 23; Culver Pictures, page 130; Lewis Hine, page 74; Student Nonviolent Coordinating Committee, pages 185, 191; Wide World Photos, pages 62, 173.

I am very grateful to Anne Grandinetti and Molly Gallon for their help in typing the manuscript.

Foreword

I*n the first and second volumes of* In Their Own Words *the story of the American Negro is told from his arrival at Jamestown in 1619 to the eve of World War I.*

This third and final volume of the series begins with the great migration from the cotton fields of the South to the big cities of the North. Through letters, memoirs, autobiographies, articles, editorials, interviews, affidavits, eyewitness accounts, and testimony given in public hearings, we come to understand the deep changes which have taken place in the Negro's life since that time. His part in two world wars, his achievements in the Negro Renaissance of the twenties, the disaster of the Great Depression, the hope offered by the New Deal and the powerful surge of unionism—all are expressed in his own words. The volume concludes with several voices speaking from the battle lines of today's Freedom Movement.

A brief introduction is provided for each document. The

date printed with each selection is not necessarily the date the document was written or published. It is sometimes the date of the period the document deals with. Several of the documents are printed in full; some are shortened, with care taken not to distort their meaning. Paragraphing and punctuation have been modernized for easier reading. Finally, to make the book as useful as possible, there is a calendar of Negro history, a reading list, and an index.

MILTON MELTZER

Contents

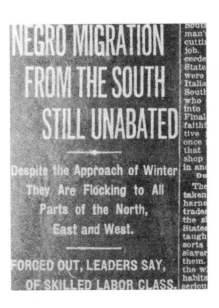

I*t began with the boll weevil.
That hungry pest crossed over from Mexico into Texas, "jes
a-lookin' for a home," and he found it in the cotton fields of
the South. By 1916 the invader, aided by storms and floods,
had ruined vast stretches of Southern land. Sharecroppers hun-
gered and shivered in their rickety cabins as landlords, too
broke to extend credit, cut off supplies. Families wondered
what to do, where to go, how to live.*

*One way out pointed North. There were jobs up there, peo-
ple said. And they let you live a little. The war that exploded
in Europe in 1914 had cut off the flow of immigrants from the
old countries. Northern factories, booming on war orders, were
short of labor. Manufacturers sent agents South to recruit Ne-*

1

gro workers. They came with free railroad passes in hand or offered cheap tickets to groups of migrants. A "Northern fever" seized the Negroes of the South. The dream of decent jobs, of a house with a floor and windows, of schools and escape from insult and humiliation, led half a million to move North in 1917-1918. Chicago was the mecca for many. The rail lines of the deep South states led straight there. And out of the big city came a powerful voice, arguing, pleading, challenging, insisting that Negroes join "The Great Northern Drive." It was Robert S. Abbott, using his Chicago Defender to penetrate every cabin and slum with a message of hope. From black hand to black hand went the tattered pages reporting in grisly detail the rising tide of Dixieland lynchings while they pictured the prosperity of Southern Negroes who had made good in the North.

Letters from Negroes—many of them illiterate scrawls from men and women desperate to learn and be free—flooded into the Defender's office, checking on rumors of the exodus, begging to know how to come. From them you can understand why so many were looking for a promised land.

I want to get out . . .

1917

Sir: I am a poor woman and have a husband and five children living and three dead one single and two twin girls six months old today and my husband can hardly make bread for them in Mobile. This is my native home but it is not fit to live in just as the Chicago *Defender* say it says the truth and my husband only get $1.50 a day and pays $7.50 a month for house rent and can hardly feed me and his self and children . . . I want to get out of this dog hold because I don't know what I am raising them up for in this place and I want to get to Chicago where I know they will be raised and my husband crazy to get there because he know he can get more to raise his children and will you please let me know where the cars is going to stop so that he can come where he can take care of me and my children. He get there a while and then he can send for me. I heard they wasn't coming here so I sent to find out and he can go and meet them at the place they are going and

3

go from there to Chicago. No more at present. hoping to hear from you soon from your needed and worried friend.

NEW ORLEANS, LA., MAY 2, 1917.
Dear Sir: Please Sir will you kindly tell me what is meant by the great Northern Drive to take place May the 15th on Tuesday. It is a rumor all over town to be ready for the 15th of May to go in the drive. the *Defender* first spoke of the drive the 10th of February. My husband is in the north already preparing for our family but hearing that the excursion will be $6.00 from here north on the 15th and having a large family, I could profit by it if it is really true. Do please write me at once and say is there an excursion to leave the south. Nearly the whole of the south is getting ready for the drive or excursion as it is termed. Please write at once. We are sick to get out of the solid south.

TROY, ALA., OCT. 17, 1916.
Dear Sirs: I am enclosing a clipping of a lynching again which speaks for itself. I do wish there could be sufficient presure brought about to have federal investigation of such work. I wrote you a few days ago if you could furnish me with the addresses of some firms or co-opporations that needed common labor. So many of our people here are almost starving . . . quite a number here would go any where to better their conditions. If you can do any thing for us write me as early as possible.

BHAM, ALA., MAY 13, 1917.
Sir: i am in the darkness of the south and i am trying my

4

best to get out do you no where about i can get a job in new york. i wood be so glad if cood get a good job . . . o please help me to get out of this low down county i am counted no more thin a dog help me please help me o how glad i wood be if some company wood send me a ticket to come and work for them no joking i mean business i work if i can get a good job.

BRYAN, TEX., SEPT. 13, 1917.
Dear Sir: I am writing you as I would like to no if you no of any R. R. Co and Mfg. that are in need for colored labors. I want to bring a bunch of race men out of the south we want work some whear north will come if we can git passe any whear across the Mason & Dickson. please let me hear from you at once if you can git passes for 10 or 12 men. send at once.

ANNISTON, ALA., APRIL 23, 1917.
Dear Sir: Please gave me some infamation about coming north i can do any kind of work from a truck gardin to farming i would like to leave here and i cant make no money to leave i ust make enought to live one please let me here from you at once i want to get where i can put my children in schol.

Dear Sir: I saw your add in the Chicago *Defender* for laborers. I am a young man and want to finish school. I want you to look out for me a job on the place working morning and evening. I would like to get a job in some private family so I could continue taking my piano lesson I can do anything around the house but drive and can even learn that. Send me the name of the best High School in Chicago. How is the Wendell Phillips College. I have finish the grammar school.

From *Journal of Negro History,* July and October, 1919.

RICHARD WRIGHT

T*o the letters of Southern Ne-
groes yearning to come North can be added the testimony of
Richard Wright. His father, a laborer, had left his mother
when Richard was very young, and at 15 the boy decided to
run away from home. His schooling had stopped in the eighth
grade. From Natchez he wandered up to Memphis, where he
worked as errand boy and as porter. "But all I really wanted
to do in those days," he said, "was to read." Up along the Mississippi he moved, finding jobs here and there until finally he
reached Chicago. "There I worked first at sweeping streets and
then at digging ditches." After a while he started to write, see-*

ing a few of his articles and stories appearing in the little literary magazines. Now it was the years of the Great Depression, and the federal government's job relief program—the Works Progress Administration—opened projects for writers, actors, artists, musicians. Richard Wright went to work on the Federal Writers Project in Chicago. In 1937 his Uncle Tom's Children *won a contest among WPA writers. In it he transformed his young years into powerful short stories. One of his early pieces was "The Ethics of Living Jim Crow," a moving memory of his youth. From it comes this section telling how a boy of those days learned to live as a Negro.*

My first lesson . . .
1917

MY FIRST LESSON in how to live
as a Negro came when I was quite small. We were living in
Arkansas. Our house stood behind the railroad tracks. Its
skimpy yard was paved with black cinders. Nothing green ever
grew in that yard. The only touch of green we could see was
far away, beyond the tracks, over where the white folks lived.
But cinders were good enough for me, and I never missed the
green growing things. And, anyhow, cinders were fine weap-
ons. You could always have a nice hot war with huge black
cinders. All you had to do was crouch behind the brick pillars
of a house with your hands full of gritty ammunition. And the
first woolly black head you saw pop out from behind another
row of pillars was your target. You tried your very best to
knock it off. It was great fun.

I never fully realized the appalling disadvantages of a cinder environment till one day the gang to which I belonged
found itself engaged in a war with the white boys who lived
beyond the tracks. As usual, we laid down our cinder barrage,
thinking that this would wipe the white boys out. But they

replied with a steady bombardment of broken bottles. We doubled our cinder barrage, but they hid behind trees, hedges, and the sloping embankments of their lawns. Having no such fortifications, we retreated to the brick pillars of our homes. During the retreat a broken milk bottle caught me behind the ear, opening a deep gash which bled profusely. The sight of blood pouring over my face completely demoralized our ranks. My fellow combatants left me standing paralyzed in the center of the yard and scurried for their homes. A kind neighbor saw me and rushed me to a doctor, who took three stitches in my neck.

I sat brooding on my front steps, nursing my wound and waiting for my mother to come from work. I felt that a grave injustice had been done me. It was all right to throw cinders. The greatest harm a cinder could do was leave a bruise. But broken bottles were dangerous; they left you cut, bleeding, and helpless.

When night fell my mother came from the white folks' kitchen. I raced down the street to meet her. I could just feel in my bones that she would understand. I knew she would tell me exactly what to do next time. I grabbed her hand and babbled out the whole story. She examined my wound, then slapped me.

"How come yuh didn't hide?" she asked me. "How come yuh always fightin'?"

I was outraged, and bawled. Between sobs I told her that I didn't have any trees or hedges to hide behind. There wasn't a thing I could have used as a trench. And you couldn't throw very far when you were hiding behind the brick pillars of a house. She grabbed a barrel stave, dragged me home, stripped me naked, and beat me till I had a fever of one hundred and two. She would smack my rump with the stave and, while the skin was still smarting, impart to me gems of Jim Crow wisdom. I was never to throw cinders any more. I was never to fight any more wars. I was never, never, under any conditions, to fight white folks again. And they were absolutely right in clouting me with the broken milk bottle. Didn't I know she was working hard every day in the hot kitchens of the white folks to make money to take care of me? When was I ever going to learn to be a good boy? She couldn't be bothered with my fights. She finished by telling me that I ought to be thankful to God as long as I lived that they didn't kill me.

All that night I was delirious and could not sleep. Each time I closed my eyes I saw monstrous white faces suspended from the ceiling, leering at me.

From that time on the charm of my cinder yard was gone. The green trees, the trimmed hedges, the cropped lawns grew very meaningful, became a symbol. Even today, when I think of white folks, the hard, sharp outlines of white houses surrounded by trees, lawns, and hedges are present somewhere in the background of my mind. Through the years they grew into an overreaching symbol of fear.

It was a long time before I came in close contact with white folks again. We moved from Arkansas to Mississippi. Here we had the good fortune not to live behind the railroad tracks or close to white neighborhoods. We lived in the very heart of the local Black Belt. There were black churches and black preachers; there were black schools and black teachers, black groceries and black clerks. In fact, everything was so solidly black that for a long time I did not even think of white folks, save in remote and vague terms. But this could not last forever. As one grows older one eats more. One's clothing costs more. When I finished grammar school I had to go to work. My mother could no longer feed and clothe me on her cooking job.

There is but one place where a black boy who knows no trade can get a job. And that's where the houses and faces are white, where the trees, lawns, and hedges are green. My first job was with an optical company in Jackson, Mississippi. The morning I applied I stood straight and neat before the boss, answering all his questions with sharp yessirs and nosirs. I was very careful to pronounce my sirs distinctly, in order that he might know that I was polite, that I knew where I was, and that I knew he was a white man. I wanted that job badly.

He looked me over as though he were examining a prize poodle. He questioned me closely about my schooling, being particularly insistent about how much mathematics I had had. He seemed very pleased when I told him I had had two years of algebra.

"Boy, how would you like to try to learn something around here?" he asked me.

"I'd like it fine, sir," I said, happy. I had visions of "working my way up." Even Negroes have those visions.

"All right," he said. "Come on."

I followed him to the small factory.

"Pease," he said to a white man of about thirty-five, "this is Richard. He's going to work for us."

Pease looked at me and nodded.

I was then taken to a white boy of about seventeen.

"Morrie, this is Richard, who's going to work for us."

"Whut yuh sayin' there, boy!" Morrie boomed at me.

"Fine!" I answered.

The boss instructed these two to help me, teach me, give me jobs to do, and let me learn what I could in my spare time.

My wages were five dollars a week.

I worked hard, trying to please. For the first month I got along O.K. Both Pease and Morrie seemed to like me. But one thing was missing. And I kept thinking about it. I was not learning anything, and nobody was volunteering to help me. Thinking they had forgotten that I was to learn something about the mechanics of grinding lenses, I asked Morrie one day to tell me about the work. He grew red.

"Whut yuh tryin' t' do, nigger, git smart?" he asked.

"Naw, I ain't tryin' t' git smart," I said.

"Well, don't, if yuh know whut's good for yuh!"

I was puzzled. Maybe he just doesn't want to help me, I thought. I went to Pease.

"Say, are you crazy, you black bastard?" Pease asked me, his gray eyes growing hard.

I spoke out, reminding him that the boss had said I was to be given a chance to learn something.

"Nigger, you think you're white, don't you?"

"Naw sir!"

"Well, you're acting mighty like it!"

"But, Mr. Pease, the boss said——"

Pease shook his fist in my face.

"This is a white man's work around here, and you better watch yourself!"

From then on they changed toward me. They said good morning no more. When I was just a bit slow in performing some duty, I was called a lazy black son-of-a-bitch.

Once I thought of reporting all this to the boss. But the mere idea of what would happen to me if Pease and Morrie should learn that I had "snitched" stopped me. And after all, the boss was a white man too. What was the use?

The climax came at noon one summer day. Pease called me to his workbench. To get to him I had to go between two narrow benches and stand with my back against a wall.

"Yes sir," I said.

"Richard, I want to ask you something," Pease began pleasantly, not looking up from his work.

"Yes sir," I said again.

Morrie came over, blocking the narrow passage between the benches. He folded his arms, staring at me solemnly.

I looked from one to the other, sensing that something was coming.

"Yes sir," I said for the third time.

Pease looked up and spoke very slowly.

"Richard, Mr. Morrie, here, tells me you called me Pease."

I stiffened. A void seemed to open up in me. I knew this was the showdown.

He meant that I had failed to call him Mr. Pease. I looked at Morrie. He was gripping a steel bar in his hands. I opened my mouth to speak, to protest, to assure Pease that I had never called him simply Pease and that I had never had any intentions of doing so, when Morrie grabbed me by the collar, ramming my head against the wall.

"Now, be careful, nigger!" snarled Morrie, baring his teeth. "I heard yuh call 'im Pease. 'N' if yuh say yuh didn't, you're callin' me a liar, see?" He waved the steel bar threateningly.

If I had said, "No sir, Mr. Pease, I never called you Pease,"

I would have been automatically calling Morrie a liar. And if I had said, "Yes sir, Mr. Pease, I called you Pease," I would have been pleading guilty to having uttered the worst insult that a Negro can utter to a Southern white man. I stood hesitating, trying to frame a neutral reply.

"Richard, I asked you a question!" said Pease. Anger was creeping into his voice.

"I don't remember calling you Pease, Mr. Pease," I said cautiously. "And if I did, I sure didn't mean——"

"You black son-of-a-bitch! You called me Pease, then!" he spat, slapping me till I bent sideways over a bench. Morrie was on top of me, demanding:

"Didn't yuh call 'im Pease? If yuh say yuh didn't I'll rip yo' gut string loose with this bar, yuh black granny dodger! Yuh can't tell a white man a lie 'n' git erway with it, you black son-of-a-bitch!"

I wilted. I begged them not to bother me. I knew what they wanted. They wanted me to leave.

"I'll leave," I promised. "I'll leave right now."

They gave me a minute to get out of the factory. I was warned not to show up again or tell the boss.

I went.

When I told the folks at home what had happened, they called me a fool. They told me that I must never again attempt to exceed my boundaries. When you are working for white folks, they said, you got to "stay in your place" if you want to keep working. . . .

From *Uncle Tom's Children,* by Richard Wright, Harper, 1938.

By 1928 almost a million and a
quarter migrants had come up from the South to find a new life
in the Northern cities. Young Richard Wright was one of them.
Born near Natchez in 1908, he spent his childhood in the Delta
region—Mississippi, Arkansas, and Tennessee. Later he came
to Chicago, too, where he learned to be a writer and became
one of the most eloquent spokesmen for his generation. In
1938 he published his first novel, Native Son, describing the
life of a young Negro in a Chicago slum. It was a great success
critically and financially. The book was soon converted into
both play and movie. The next year he published 12 Million
Black Voices, a "folk history." From it comes this passage in
which Wright tells what the great exodus from the South was
like and what the migrants found when they arrived on the
pavements of the city.

The one-room kitchenette...

1917

LORD IN HEAVEN! Good God Almighty! Great Day in the Morning! Our time has come! We are leaving! We are angry no more; we are leaving! We are bitter no more; we are leaving! We are leaving our homes, pulling up stakes to move on. We look up at the high southern sky and remember all the sunshine and the rain and we feel a sense of loss, but we are leaving. We look out at the wide green fields which our eyes saw when we first came into the world and we feel full of regret, but we are leaving. We scan the kind black faces we have looked upon since we first saw the light of day, and, though pain is in our hearts, we are leaving. We take one last furtive look over our shoulders to the Big House—high upon a hill beyond the railroad tracks—where the Lord of the Land lives, and we feel glad, for we are leaving. . . .

Night and day, in rain and in sun, in winter and in summer, we leave the land. Already, as we sit and look broodingly out over the turning fields, we notice with attention and hope that the dense southern swamps give way to broad, cultivated wheat farms. The spick-and-span farmhouses done in red and green

16

and white crowd out the casual, unpainted gingerbread shacks. Silos take the place of straggling piles of hay. Macadam highways now wind over the horizon instead of dirt roads. The cheeks of the farm people are full and ruddy, not sunken and withered like soda crackers. . . .

We see white men and women get on the train, dressed in expensive new clothes. We look at them guardedly and wonder will they bother us. Will they ask us to stand up while they sit down? Will they tell us to go to the back of the coach? Even though we have been told that we need not be afraid, we have lived so long in fear of all white faces that we cannot help but sit and wait. We look around the train and we do not see the old familiar signs: FOR COLORED and FOR WHITE. The train speeds north and we cannot sleep. Our heads sink in a doze, and then we sit bolt-upright, prodded by the thought that we must watch these strange surroundings. But nothing happens; these white men seem impersonal and their very neutrality reassures us—for a while. Almost against our deeper judgment, we try to force ourselves to relax, for these brisk men give no sign of what they feel. They are indifferent. O sweet and welcome indifference!

The miles click behind us. Into Chicago, Indianapolis, New York, Cleveland, Buffalo, Detroit, Toledo, Philadelphia, Pittsburgh, and Milwaukee we go, looking for work. We feel freer than we have ever felt before, but we are still a little scared. It is like a dream. Will we wake up suddenly and find that none of this is really true, that we are merely daydreaming behind the barn, snoozing in the sun, waiting to hear the hoarse voice of the riding boss saying: "Nigger, where do you think you are? Get the hell up from there and move on!"

Timidly, we get off the train. We hug our suitcases, fearful of pickpockets, looking with unrestrained curiosity at the great big brick buildings. We are very reserved, for we have been warned not to act "green," that the city people can spot a "sucker" a mile away. Then we board our first Yankee street car to go to a cousin's home, a brother's home, a sister's home, a friend's home, an uncle's home or an aunt's home. We pay the conductor our fare and look about apprehensively for a seat. We have been told that we can sit where we please, but we are still scared. We cannot shake off three hundred years of fear in three hours. We ease into a seat and look out of the window at the crowded streets. A white man or a white woman comes and sits beside us, not even looking at us, as though this were a normal thing to do. The muscles of our bodies tighten. Indefinable sensations crawl over our skins and our blood tingles. Out of the corners of our eyes we try to get a glimpse of the strange white face that floats but a few inches from ours. The impulses to laugh and to cry clash in us; we bite our lips and stare out of the window.

There are so many people. For the first time in our lives we feel human bodies, strangers whose lives and thoughts are unknown to us, pressing always close about us. We cannot see or know a man because of the thousands upon thousands of men. The apartments in which we sleep are crowded and noisy, and soon enough we learn that the brisk, clipped men of the North, the Bosses of the Buildings, are not at all indifferent. They are deeply concerned about us, but in a new way. It seems as though we are now living inside of a machine; days and events move with a hard reasoning of their own. We live amid swarms of people, yet there is a vast distance between people, a distance that words cannot bridge. No longer do our lives depend upon the soil, the sun, the rain, or the wind; we live by the grace of jobs and the brutal logic of jobs. We do not know this world, or what makes it move. In the South life was different; men spoke to you, cursed you, yelled at you, or killed you. The world moved by signs we knew. But here in the North cold forces hit you and push you. It is a world of things.

Our defenseless eyes cloud with bewilderment when we learn that there are not enough houses for us to live in. And competing with us for shelter are thousands of poor migrant whites who have come up from the South, just as we have come. The cost of building a house is high, and building activities are on the downgrade. It is wartime; no new labor is coming in from the old countries across the seas. The only district we can live in is the area just beyond the business belt, a transition area where a sooty conglomeration of factories and mills belches smoke that stains our clothes and lungs. . . .

Having been warned against us by the Bosses of the Buildings, having heard tall tales about us, about how "bad" we are, they (the whites) react emotionally as though we had the plague when we move into their neighborhoods. Is it any wonder, then, that their homes are suddenly and drastically reduced in value? They hastily abandon them, sacrificing them to the Bosses of the Buildings, the men who instigate all this for whatever profit they can get in real-estate sales. And in the end we are all the "fall guys." When the white folks move, the Bosses of the Buildings let the property to us at rentals higher than those the whites paid.

And the Bosses of the Buildings take these old houses and

convert them into "kitchenettes," and then rent them to us at rates so high that they make fabulous fortunes before the houses are too old for habitation. What they do is this: they take, say, a seven-room apartment, which rents for $50 a month to whites, and cut it up into seven small apartments, of one room each; they install one small gas stove and one small sink in each room. The Bosses of the Buildings rent these kitchenettes to us at the rate of, say, $6 a week. Hence, the same apartment for which white people—who can get jobs anywhere and who receive higher wages than we—pay $50 a month is rented to us for $42 a week! And because there are not enough houses for us to live in, because we have been used to sleeping several in a room on the plantations in the South, we rent these kitchenettes and are glad to get them. These kitchenettes are our havens from the plantations in the South. We have fled the wrath of Queen Cotton and we are tired.

Sometimes five or six of us live in a one-room kitchenette, a place where simple folk such as we should never be held captive. A war sets up in our emotions: one part of our feelings tells us that it is good to be in the city, that we have a chance at life here, that we need but turn a corner to become a stranger, that we no longer need bow and dodge at the sight of the Lords of the Land. Another part of our feelings tells us that, in terms of worry and strain, the cost of living in the kitchenettes is too high, that the city heaps too much responsibility upon us and gives too little security in return.

The kitchenette is the author of the glad tidings that new suckers are in town, ready to be cheated, plundered, and put in their places.

The kitchenette is our prison, our death sentence without

a trial, the new form of mob violence that assaults not only the lone individual, but all of us, in its ceaseless attacks.

The kitchenette, with its filth and foul air, with its one toilet for thirty or more tenants, kills our black babies so fast that in many cities twice as many of them die as white babies.

The kitchenette is the seed bed for scarlet fever, dysentery, typhoid, tuberculosis, gonorrhea, syphilis, pneumonia, and malnutrition.

The kitchenette scatters death so widely among us that our death rate exceeds our birth rate, and if it were not for the trains and autos bringing us daily into the city from the plantations, we black folks who dwell in northern cities would die out entirely over the course of a few years.

The kitchenette, with its crowded rooms and incessant bedlam, provides an enticing place for crimes of all sort—crimes against women and children or any stranger who happens to stray into its dark hallways. The noise of our living, boxed in stone and steel, is so loud that even a pistol shot is smothered.

The kitchenette throws desperate and unhappy people into an unbearable closeness of association, thereby increasing latent friction, giving birth to never-ending quarrels of recrimination, accusation, and vindictiveness, producing warped personalities.

The kitchenette injects pressure and tension into our individual personalities, making many of us give up the struggle, walk off and leave wives, husbands, and even children behind to shift as best they can.

The kitchenette creates thousands of one-room homes where our black mothers sit deserted, with their children about their knees.

The kitchenette blights the personalities of our growing children, disorganizes them, blinds them to hope, creates problems whose effects can be traced in the characters of its child victims for years afterward.

The kitchenette jams our farm girls, while still in their teens, into rooms with men who are restless and stimulated by the noise and lights of the city; and more of our girls have bastard babies than the girls in any other sections of the city.

The kitchenette fills our black boys with longing and restlessness, urging them to run off from home, to join together with other restless black boys in gangs, that brutal form of city courage.

The kitchenette piles up mountains of profits for the Bosses of the Buildings and makes them ever more determined to keep things as they are.

The kitchenette reaches out with fingers full of golden bribes to the officials of the city, persuading them to allow old firetraps to remain standing and occupied long after they should have been torn down.

The kitchenette is the funnel through which our pulverized lives flow to ruin and death on the city pavements, at a profit. . . .

From *12 Million Black Voices,* by Richard Wright
and Edwin Rosskam, Viking Press, 1941.

369TH INFANTRY REGIMENT MARCHING UP FIFTH AVENUE
ON ITS RETURN FROM FRANCE IN 1919

A*s the wartime industries
grew, more and more Negroes rushed North in the hope of
finding work. Many got jobs better than anything they had
known before. They found a place in iron and steel mills, in
meatpacking and auto plants; they helped build ships and mine
coal and run railroads. But their problems in the crowded
black ghettoes multiplied with their numbers. White workers
feared their competition on the job and tried to keep them
out of their neighborhoods. The government offered no protection against discrimination and segregation. For a while
Negroes had put their faith in Woodrow Wilson's 1912 campaign promise to see "justice done to the colored people in*

every matter." But once in office, the Virginia-born President strung Jim Crow fences throughout the federal government.

In 1917 the United States entered World War I—"to make the world safe for democracy," President Wilson said. The world did not seem to include the American Negro. The same Jim Crow fence cut across the armed forces, where 367,000 Negroes served. The new Air Corps slammed the door tight against blacks; the Navy rated them fit for menial duty only; and the other armed services segregated them. There were clashes between Negro and white soldiers in the training camps and between Negro soldiers and white civilians in the communities surrounding them. When the colored troops reached France, believed to be a prejudice-free haven, they found the Army had warned the French not to treat Negro soldiers as equals. Nevertheless, Negroes made a great record in combat, winning many citations for bravery. Perhaps some felt that with all the wartime talk of democracy surely things would be different when they got home.

As the packed troopships crossed the Atlantic homeward bound, Dr. W. E. B. DuBois put in words the feeling in the hearts of the Negro soldiers. He published those words in 1919 in The Crisis, *the journal he edited for the National Association for the Advancement of Colored People.*

Born in 1868, DuBois was now 51. He was one of America's foremost scholars, but never content to float quietly in an academic backwater. He was fearless in his leadership of the Negro protest movement and through his writings had an enormous influence on his own generation and on all those that have followed.

We return—fighting! . . .

1919

WE ARE RETURNING from war! *The Crisis* and tens of thousands of black men were drafted into a great struggle. For bleeding France and what she means and has meant and will mean to us and humanity and against the threat of German race arrogance, we fought gladly and to the last drop of blood; for America and her highest ideals, we fought in far-off hope; for the dominant southern oligarchy entrenched in Washington, we fought in bitter resignation. For the America that represents and gloats in lynching, disfranchisement, caste, brutality and devilish insult—for this, in the hateful upturning and mixing of things, we were forced by vindictive fate to fight, also.

But today we return! We return from slavery of uniform which the world's madness demanded us to don to the freedom of civil garb. We stand again to look America squarely in the face and call a spade a spade. We sing: This country of ours, despite all its better souls have done and dreamed, is yet a shameful land.

It lynches.

And lynching is barbarism of a degree of contemptible nastiness unparalleled in human history. Yet for fifty years we have lynched two Negroes a week, and we have kept this up right through the war.

It disfranchises its own citizens.

Disfranchisement is the deliberate theft and robbery of the only protection of poor against rich and black against white. The land that disfranchises its citizens and calls itself a democracy lies and knows it lies.

It encourages ignorance.

It has never really tried to educate the Negro. A dominant minority does not want Negroes educated. It wants servants, dogs, whores and monkeys. And when this land allows a reactionary group by its stolen political power to force as many black folk into these categories as it possibly can, it cries in contemptible hypocrisy: "They threaten us with degeneracy; they cannot be educated."

It steals from us.

It organizes industry to cheat us. It cheats us out of our land; it cheats us out of our labor. It confiscates our savings. It reduces our wages. It raises our rent. It steals our profit. It taxes us without representation. It keeps us consistently and universally poor, and then feeds us on charity and derides our poverty.

It insults us.

It has organized a nation-wide and latterly a worldwide propaganda of deliberate and continuous insult and defamation of black blood wherever found. It decrees that it shall not be possible in travel nor residence, work nor play, education nor instruction for a black man to exist without tacit or open acknowledgment of his inferiority to the dirtiest white dog. And it looks upon any attempt to question or even discuss this dogma as arrogance, unwarranted assumption and treason.

This is the country to which we Soldiers of Democracy return. This is the fatherland for which we fought! But it is our fatherland. It was right for us to fight. The faults of our country are our faults. Under similar circumstances, we would fight again. But by the God of Heaven, we are cowards and jackasses if now that that war is over, we do not marshal every ounce of our brain and brawn to fight a sterner, longer, more unbending battle against the forces of hell in our own land.

We return.

We return from fighting.

We return fighting.

Make way for Democracy! We saved it in France, and by the Great Jehovah, we will save it in the United States of America, or know the reason why.

From *The Crisis,* 1919.

That summer of 1919 they called "The Red Summer." Red for blood. It was the first postwar year, but as the returning Negro troops stepped off the ships, they walked into another war. In Mississippi mobs killed three Negro soldiers, in Georgia another three, in Arkansas two, in Florida one, in Alabama, another. Still in their uniforms, they were lynched. In a year, 70 Negroes died at the hands of murdering mobs. Between June and December the records show 25 race riots in cities from one end of the country to the other.

Chicago, "top of the world" to the Southern migrant, saw the worst racial outbreak in 1919. It began July 27 and raged up and down the streets for several days and nights. The city lay helpless under the warring mobs. When it was at last ended, over 500 persons had been injured and 38 killed. A thousand families lost their homes to fire and destruction.

The NAACP sought the facts. What could explain the most savage race war the nation had yet seen? The man chosen to investigate Chicago was Walter White, then assistant secretary of the NAACP. He was often to go on these dangerous missions, penetrating to the deepest South because he was blond and blue-eyed and could "pass." The son of an Atlanta mail carrier, at the age of 13 he had been caught with his father in the 1906 race riot in which a dozen Negroes died. The two escaped because the mob thought they were whites. The next day, with guns in hand, they and their neighbors successfully defended their homes from the torches of rioters.

The month White spent probing for the causes of the Chicago riot brought to light several fundamental facts which he reported in The Crisis. Much the same could be written about all the race riots that have occurred in the half-century since that day.

Riot in Chicago . . .

1919

MANY CAUSES HAVE been as-
signed for the three days of race rioting. . . . Charges and
counter-charges are made, but, as is usually the case, the Negro
is made to bear the brunt of it all—to be "the scapegoat." A
background of strained race relations brought . . . the for-
mation of a situation where only a spark was needed to ignite
the flames of racial antagonism. That spark was contributed
by a white youth when he knocked a colored lad off a raft at
the 29th Street bathing beach and the colored boy was
drowned.

Four weeks spent in studying the situation in Chicago, immediately following the outbreaks, seem to show at least eight
general causes for the riots, and the same conditions, to a
greater or less degree, can be found in almost every large city
with an appreciable Negro population. These causes, taken
after a careful study in order of their prominence, are:

1 Race Prejudice.
2 Economic Competition.
3 Political Corruption and Exploitation of Negro Voters.
4 Police Inefficiency.
5 Newspaper Lies about Negro Crime.
6 Unpunished Crimes Against Negroes.
7 Housing.
8 Reaction of Whites and Negroes from War.

Some of these can be grouped under the same headings, but due to the prominence of each they are listed as separate causes.

Prior to 1915, Chicago had been famous for its remarkably fair attitude toward colored citizens. Since that time, when the migratory movement from the South assumed large proportions, the situation has steadily grown more and more tense. This was due in part to the introduction of many Negroes who were unfamiliar with city ways and could not, naturally, adapt themselves immediately to their new environment. . . .

But equally important, though seldom considered, is the fact that many Southern whites have also come into the North, many of them to Chicago, drawn by the same economic advantages that attracted the colored workman. . . . These have spread the virus of race hatred and evidences of it can be seen in Chicago on every hand. This same cause underlies each of the other seven causes.

With regard to economic competition, the age-long dispute between capital and labor enters. Large numbers of Negroes were brought from the South by the packers and there is little doubt that this was done in part so that the Negro might be used as a club over the heads of the unions. . . . On the other hand, the Negro workman is not at all sure as to the sincerity of the unions themselves. The Negro in Chicago yet remembers the waiters' strike some years ago, when colored union workers walked out at the command of the unions and when the strike was settled, the unions did not insist that Negro waiters be given their jobs back along with whites, and, as a result, colored men have never been able to get back into some of the hotels even to the present day. . . .

With the possible exception of Philadelphia, there is probably no city in America with more of political trickery, chicanery and exploitation than Chicago. . . .

The fourth contributing cause was the woeful inefficiency and criminal negligence of the police authorities of Chicago both prior to and during the riots. Prostitution, gambling and the illicit sale of whiskey flourish openly and apparently without any fear whatever of police interference. . . .

All of this tended to contribute to open disregard for law and almost contempt for it. Due either to political "pull" or to reciprocal arrangements, many notorious dives run and policemen are afraid to arrest the proprietors.

During the riots the conduct of the police force as a whole was equally open to criticism. State's Attorney Hoyne openly charged the police with arresting colored rioters and with an unwillingness to arrest white rioters. Those who were arrested were at once released. . . .

Fifth on the list is the effect of newspaper publicity concerning Negro crime. With the exception of the *Daily News,* all of the papers of Chicago have played up in prominent style with glaring, prejudice-breeding headlines every crime or suspected crime committed by Negroes. Headlines such as

"NEGRO BRUTALLY MURDERS PROMINENT CITI-ZEN," "NEGRO ROBS HOUSE" and the like have appeared with alarming frequency and the news articles beneath such headlines have been of the same sort. During the rioting such headlines as "NEGRO BANDITS TERRORIZE TOWN," "RIOTERS BURN 100 HOMES—NEGROES SUSPECTED OF HAVING PLOTTED BLAZE" appeared. In the latter case a story was told of witnesses seeing Negroes in automobiles applying torches and fleeing. This was the story given to the press by Fire Attorney John R. McCabe after a casual and hasty survey. Later the office of State Fire Marshal Gamber proved conclusively that the fires were not caused by Negroes but by whites. As can easily be seen such newspaper accounts did not tend to lessen the bitterness of feeling between the conflicting groups. Further, many wild and unfounded rumors were published in the press—incendiary and inflammatory to the highest degree. . . .

For a long period prior to the riots, organized gangs of white hoodlums had been perpetrating crimes against Negroes for which no arrests had been made. These gangs in many instances masqueraded under the name of "Athletic and Social Clubs" and later direct connection was shown between them and incendiary fires started during the riots. Colored men, women and children had been beaten in the parks. . . . In one case a young colored girl was beaten and thrown into a lagoon. In other cases Negroes were beaten so severely that they had to be taken to hospitals. All of these cases had caused many colored people to wonder if they could expect any protection whatever from the authorities. . . .

Much has been written and said concerning the housing

situation in Chicago and its effect on the racial situation. The problem is a simple one. Since 1915 the colored population of Chicago has more than doubled, increasing in four years from a little over 50,000 to what is now estimated to be between 125,000 and 150,000. . . . Already overcrowded, this so-called "Black Belt" could not possibly hold the doubled colored population. One cannot put ten gallons of water in a five-gallon pail.

Although many Negroes had been living in "white" neighborhoods, the increased exodus from the old areas created an hysterical group of persons who formed "Property Owners' Associations" for the purpose of keeping intact white neighborhoods. . . . Early in June the writer, while in Chicago, attended a private meeting. . . . Various plans were discussed for keeping the Negroes in "their part of the town," such as securing the discharge of colored persons from positions they held when they attempted to move into "white" neighborhoods, purchasing mortgages of Negroes buying homes and ejecting them when mortgage notes fell due and were unpaid, and many more of the same calibre. The language of many speakers was vicious and strongly prejudicial and had the distinct effect of creating race bitterness.

In a number of cases, during the period from January 1918 to August 1919, there were bombings of colored homes and houses occupied by Negroes outside of the "Black Belt." During this period no less than twenty bombings took place, yet only two persons have been arrested and neither of the two has been convicted, both cases continued.

Finally, the new spirit aroused in Negroes by their war experiences enters into the problem. . . . These men, with

their new outlook on life, injected the same spirit of independence into their companions, a thing that is true of many
other sections of America. One of the greatest surprises to
many of those who came down to "clean out the niggers" is
that these same "niggers" fought back. Colored men saw their
own kind being killed, heard of many more and believed that
their lives and liberty were at stake. In such a spirit most of the
fighting was done.

From *The Crisis,* October 1919.

MARCUS GARVEY

Among the thousands of immigrants from the West Indies to Harlem in 1916 was a chunky black Jamaican named Marcus Garvey. Two years earlier, in his native island, he had started the Universal Negro Improvement Association. On the sidewalks of New York his talk about redeeming the race made little impression at first. Garvey wandered west from Harlem, touring 38 states to see how the Negro lived in America. Everywhere he found tens of thousands of migrants from the South jammed into rickety tenements, Jim Crowed on their jobs and in their neighborhoods, living in the shadow of the big white world and living on its castoffs.

For a few years he made little progress in winning the Negro masses with his message—pride in race. But neither had any other organization made headway with the Negro people. The National Urban League and the NAACP had paid more attention to middle-class than working-class Negroes, and depended upon better-off whites and Negroes for support. But by 1919, the year in which race riots erupted in a deadly rash over the face of America, the Negroes were ready for a program that pointed a way out of the prison of the ghetto. Marcus Garvey had the gifts to dramatize his dream of a black world ruled by black men. The Negro should be proud of his past, he said, proud of the great empires built by black men in Africa's glorious age, proud of his very blackness. Garvey praised everything black. The color was a sign of strength and beauty, he said, not a badge of inferiority.

In his speeches and his newspaper, The Negro World, *he declared the white man's prejudice against the black was so strong it was foolish to believe his sermons on justice and democracy would ever mean anything in practice. This America was a white man's country, he said, and no place for a Negro. The only hope for the Negro was to build an independent nation in Africa, the ancestral homeland.*

Garvey's black nationalist appeal showed amazing success by 1919. The UNIA grew swiftly, its branches spreading to most of the large centers of Negro population. Garvey gave his followers parades and pageants, uniforms and titles, conventions and conferences. By the mid-twenties, he had about a million followers. He organized stores, factories, cooperatives, and a Black Star Steamship Line. It was this last venture that ended his sensational rise. It showed a heavy financial loss and Garvey was tried for fraud. Found guilty, he was sent to prison in 1925. Two years later, he was pardoned, but deported as an alien. He lived the rest of his life in obscurity.

Garvey never reached Africa, nor did he ever land any of his followers on that shore. But that was no measure of Garveyism's meaning. It was the first real mass movement among American Negroes in the country's history. Negroes showed they did not want to leave the United States any more than had earlier generations, no matter how angry and bitter they were. What Garvey did was to strengthen their self-respect and pride, to open out the world to them, to show the promise of liberation which the African nations would achieve a generation later.

From Garvey's writings comes this statement of his ideas and beliefs.

Black men,
you shall be
great again . . .
1923

IT COMES TO THE individual, the race, the nation, once in a lifetime to decide upon the course to be pursued as a career. The hour has now struck for the individual Negro as well as the entire race to decide the course that will be pursued in the interest of our own liberty.

We who make up the Universal Negro Improvement Association have decided that we shall go forward, upward and onward toward the great goal of human liberty. We have determined among ourselves that all barriers placed in the way of our progress must be removed, must be cleared away for we desire to see the light of a brighter day.

The Universal Negro Improvement Association for five years has been proclaiming to the world the readiness of the Negro to carve out a pathway for himself in the course of life. . . . We are organized for the absolute purpose of bettering our condition, industrially, commercially, socially, religiously and politically. We are organized not to hate other men, but to lift ourselves, and to demand respect of all humanity. We have a program that we believe to be righteous; we believe it to be just, and we have made up our minds to lay down ourselves on the altar of sacrifice for the realization of this great hope of ours, based upon the foundation of righteousness. We declare to the world that Africa must be free, that the entire Negro race must be emancipated from industrial bondage, peonage and serfdom; we make no compromise, we make no apology in this our declaration. We do not desire to create offense on the part of the other races, but we are determined that we shall be heard, that we shall be given the rights to which we are entitled. . . .

Men of the Negro race, let me say to you that a greater future is in store for us; we have no cause to lose hope, to become faint-hearted. We must realize that upon ourselves depend our destiny, our future; we must carve out that future, that destiny, and we who make up the Universal Negro Improvement Association have pledged ourselves that nothing in the world shall stand in our way, nothing in the world shall discourage us, but opposition shall make us work harder, shall bring us closer together so that as one man the millions of us will march on toward the goal that we have set for ourselves.

The new Negro shall not be deceived. The new Negro refuses to take advice from anyone who has not felt with him, and suffered with him. We have suffered for three hundred years, therefore we feel that the time has come when only those who have suffered with us can interpret our feelings and our spirit. It takes the slave to interpret the feelings of the slave; it takes the unfortunate man to interpret the spirit of his unfortunate brother; and so it takes the suffering Negro to interpret the spirit of his comrade. . . .

There is many a leader of our race who tells us that everything is well, and that all things will work out themselves and that a better day is coming. Yes, all of us know that a better day is coming; we all know that one day we will go home to Paradise, but whilst we are hoping by our Christian virtues to have an entry into Paradise we also realize that we are living on earth, and that the things that are practised in Paradise are not practiced here. You have to treat this world as the world treats you; we are living in a temporal, material age, an age of activity, an age of racial, national selfishness. What else can you expect but to give back to the world what the world gives to you, and we are calling upon the four hundred million Negroes of the world to take a decided stand, a determined stand, that we shall occupy a firm position; that position shall be an emancipated race and a free nation of our own. We are determined that we shall have a free country; we are determined that we shall have a flag; we are determined that we shall have a government second to none in the world. . . .

When we come to consider the history of man, was not the Negro a power, was he not great once? Yes, honest students of history can recall the day when Egypt, Ethiopia and Timbuctoo towered in their civilizations, towered above Europe, towered above Asia. When Europe was inhabited by a race of cannibals, a race of savages, naked men, heathens and pagans, Africa was peopled with a race of cultured black men, who were masters in art, science and literature; men who were cultured and refined; men who, it was said, were like the gods. Even the great poets of old sang in beautiful sonnets of the delight it afforded the gods to be in companionship with the Ethiopians. Why, then, should we lose hope? Black men, you

41

were once great; you shall be great again. Lose not courage, lose not faith, go forward. The thing to do is to get organized; keep separated and you will be exploited, you will be robbed, you will be killed. Get organized, and you will compel the world to respect you. If the world fails to give you consideration, because you are black men, because you are Negroes, four hundred millions of you shall, through organization, shake the pillars of the universe and bring down creation, even as Samson brought down the temple upon his head and upon the heads of the Philistines.

So Negroes, I say, through the Universal Negro Improvement Association, that there is much to live for. I have a vision of the future, and I see before me a picture of a redeemed Africa, with her dotted cities, with her beautiful civilization, with her millions of happy children, going to and fro. Why should I lose hope, why should I give up and take a back place in this age of progress? Remember that you are men, that God created you Lords of this creation. Lift up yourselves, men, take yourselves out of the mire and hitch your hopes to the stars; yes, rise as high as the very stars themselves. Let no man pull you down, let no man destroy your ambition, because man is but your companion, your equal; man is your brother; he is not your lord; he is not your sovereign master. . . .

From *Philosophy and Opinions of Marcus Garvey,*
Universal Publishing House, 1923.

LANGSTON HUGHES

Harlem in the 1920s was the largest Negro community in the world. The tide of migration flowing North from countryside to city had in one decade deposited a rich human soil out of which was growing the "New Negro." That was what they were calling the younger generation. In the process of being transplanted, as the scholar Alain Locke put it, the Negro was becoming transformed. Behind the migration were the boll weevil, the demand for labor, the terror of the Ku Klux Klan. But more deeply, he said, lay the pull of "a new vision of opportunity, of social and economic freedom." It was a flight "from medieval America to modern."

In the big cities of the North, Negroes from everywhere—the Southern town and country, the West Indies, Africa—came together. There was a common ground to meet on where a fusing of feeling and experience took place. And a common consciousness took shape. Harlem became the race capital, the forum for expression of a developing race pride. Fresh from foreign battlefields, young Negroes were learning to fight for freedom on the home front, as well. A mood of defiance and impatience took hold. The great gap between the American creed and the American practice was given tongue by many Negro writers. They found encouragement from white editors and publishers who had begun to show interest in the country's social and economic problems. And in both The Crisis and the Urban's League's Opportunity Negro editors gave warm welcome to the poetry and prose of the new voices.

One of the strongest young voices was Langston Hughes's. At 19 he arrived in New York after a childhood and youth spent in the midwest—Missouri, Kansas, Illinois, Ohio. In this recollection of his discovery of Harlem he kaleidoscopes the years of the Harlem Renaissance.

In love with Harlem . . .

1920s

ON A BRIGHT September morning in 1921, I came up out of the subway at 135th and Lenox into the beginnings of the Negro Renaissance. I headed for the Harlem Y.M.C.A. down the block, where so many new, young, dark, male arrivals in Harlem have spent early days. The next place I headed to that afternoon was the Harlem Branch Library just up the street. There, a warm and wonderful librarian, Miss Ernestine Rose, white, made newcomers feel welcome, as did her assistant in charge of the Schomburg Collection, Catherine Latimer, a luscious café au lait. That night I went to the Lincoln Theatre across Lenox Avenue where maybe one of the Smiths—Bessie, Clara, Trixie, or Mamie— was singing the blues. And as soon as I could I made a beeline for *Shuffle Along,* the all-colored hit musical playing on 63rd Street in which Florence Mills came to fame.

I had come to New York to enter Columbia College as a freshman, but really why I had come to New York was to see Harlem. I found it hard a week or so later to tear myself away from Harlem when it came time to move up the hill to the dormitory at Columbia. That winter I spent as little time as possible on the campus. Instead, I spent as much time as I could in Harlem, and this I have done ever since. I was in love with Harlem long before I got there, and I still am in love with it. Everybody seemed to make me welcome. The sheer dark size of Harlem intrigued me. And the fact that at that time poets and writers like James Weldon Johnson and Jessie Fauset lived there, and Bert Williams, Duke Ellington, Ethel Waters, and Walter White, too, fascinated me. Had I been a rich young man, I would have bought a house in Harlem and built musical steps up to the front door, and installed chimes that at the press of a button played Ellington tunes.

After a winter at Columbia, I moved back down to Harlem. Everywhere I roomed, I had the good fortune to have lovely landladies. If I did not like a landlady's looks, I would not move in with her, maybe that is why. But at finding work in New York, my fortune was less than good. Finally, I went to sea—Africa, Europe—then a year in Paris working in a night club where the band was from Harlem. I was a dishwasher, later bus boy, listening every night to the music of Harlem transplanted to Montmartre. And I was on hand to welcome Bricktop when she came to sing for the first time in Europe, bringing with her news of Harlem.

When I came back to New York in 1925 the Negro Renaissance was in full swing. Countee Cullen was publishing his early poems, Aaron Douglas was painting, Zora Neale Hurston, Rudolph Fisher, Jean Toomer, and Wallace Thurman were writing, Louis Armstrong was playing, Cora La Redd was dancing, and the Savoy Ballroom was open with a specially built floor that rocked as the dancers swayed. Alain Locke was putting together *The New Negro*. Art took heart from Harlem creativity. Jazz filled the night air—but not everywhere—and people came from all around after dark to look upon our city within a city, Black Harlem. Had I not had to earn a living, I might have thought it even more wonderful than it was. But I could not eat the poems I wrote. Unlike the whites who came to spend their money in Harlem, only a few Harlemites seemed to live in even a modest degree of luxury. Most rode the subway downtown every morning to work or to look for work.

Downtown! I soon learned that it was seemingly impossible for black Harlem to live without white downtown. My youthful illusion that Harlem was a world unto itself did not last very long. It was not even an area that ran itself. The famous night clubs were owned by whites, as were the theatres. Almost all the stores were owned by whites, and many at that time did not even (in the very middle of Harlem) employ Negro clerks. The books of Harlem writers all had to be published downtown, if they were to be published at all. Downtown: white. Uptown: black. White downtown pulling all the strings in Harlem. Moe Gale, Moe Gale, Moe Gale, Lew Leslie, Lew Leslie, Lew Leslie, Harper's, Knopf, *The Survey Graphic,* the Harmon Foundation, the racketeers who kidnapped Casper Holstein and began to take over the numbers for whites. Negroes could not even play their own numbers with their own people. And almost all the policemen in Harlem were white. Negroes couldn't even get graft from themselves for themselves by themselves. Black Harlem really was in white face, economically speaking. So I wrote this poem:

Because my mouth
Is wide with laughter
And my throat
Is deep with song,
You do not think
I suffer after
I have held my pain
So long?

Because my mouth
Is wide with laughter,
You do not hear
My inner cry?
Because my feet
Are gay with dancing,
You do not know
I die?

Harlem, like a Picasso painting in his cubistic period. Harlem—Southern Harlem—the Carolinas, Georgia, Florida—looking for the Promised Land—dressed in rhythmic words, painted in bright pictures, dancing to jazz—and ending up in the subway at morning rush time—headed downtown. West Indian Harlem—warm rambunctious sassy remembering Marcus Garvey. Haitian Harlem, Cuban Harlem, little pockets of tropical dreams in alien tongues. Magnet Harlem, pulling an Arthur Schomburg from Puerto Rico, pulling an Arna Bontemps all the way from California, a Nora Holt from way out West, an E. Simms Campbell from St. Louis, likewise a Josephine Baker, a Charles S. Johnson from Virginia, an A. Philip Randolph from Florida, a Roy Wilkins from Minnesota, an Alta Douglas from Kansas. Melting pot Harlem—Harlem of honey and chocolate and caramel and rum and vinegar and lemon and lime and gall. Dusky dream Harlem rumbling into a nightmare tunnel where the subway from the Bronx keeps right on downtown, where the money from the nightclubs goes right on back downtown, where the jazz is drained to Broadway, whence Josephine goes to Paris, Robeson to London, Jean Toomer to a Quaker Meeting House, Garvey to the Atlanta Federal Penitentiary, and Wallace Thurman to his grave; but Duke Ellington to fame and fortune, Lena Horne to Broadway, and Buck Clayton to China.

Before it was over—our NEW NEGRO RENAISSANCE —poems became placards: Don't buy where you can't work! Adam Powell with a picket sign; me, too. BUY BLACK! Sufi long before the Black Muslims. FIRST TO BE FIRED, LAST TO BE HIRED! The Stock Market crash. The bank failures. Empty pockets. God Bless The Child That's Got His Own. Depression, Federal Theatre in Harlem, the making of Orson Welles, WPA, CCC, the Blue Eagle, Father Divine. In the midst of the Depression I got a cable from Russia inviting me to work on a motion picture there. I went to Moscow. That was the end of the early days of Langston Hughes in Harlem.

From *Freedomways,* Summer, 1963.

W. E. B. DUBOIS

R_{eaders} *who wanted to find the most pungent expression of Negro protest in the 1920s could rely upon the editorial pages of* The Crisis. *Started in 1910 as one of the first projects of the new NAACP, by 1918 its editor W. E. B. DuBois had built it to a monthly circulation of 100,000. Every question, every issue, every problem of concern to the Negro was debated in its columns.*

Before he came to The Crisis *DuBois had made many major contributions to scholarship. His Harvard doctoral thesis, on the suppression of the African slave trade, was the first publication of the world-renowned Harvard Historical Series. Later, while teaching at the University of Pennsylvania, he wrote a study of the Philadelphia Negro which pioneered in the scientific approach to the infant discipline of sociology. While a professor at Atlanta University, he edited its famous Studies of the Negro Problem.*

In the editor's chair at The Crisis, *DuBois peeled back the idiocies of racism with knife-edged irony. Here is one example from his writings of 1922.*

On being crazy . . .

1922

IT WAS ONE o'clock and I was hungry. I walked into a restaurant, seated myself and reached for the bill-of-fare. My table companion rose.

"Sir," said he, "do you wish to force your company on those who do not want you?"

No, said I, I wish to eat.

"Are you aware, sir, that this is social equality?"

Nothing of the sort, sir, it is hunger—and I ate.

The day's work done, I sought the theatre. As I sank into my seat, the lady shrank and squirmed.

I beg pardon, I said.

"Do you enjoy being where you are not wanted?" she asked coldly.

Oh no, I said.

"Well you are not wanted here."

I was surprised. I fear you are mistaken, I said. I certainly want the music and I like to think the music wants me to listen to it.

"Usher," said the lady, "this is social equality."

No, madame, said the usher, it is the second movement of Beethoven's Fifth Symphony.

After the theatre, I sought the hotel where I had sent my baggage. The clerk scowled.

"What do you want?" he asked.

Rest, I said.

"This is a white hotel," he said.

I looked around. Such a color scheme requires a great deal of cleaning, I said, but I don't know that I object.

"We object," said he.

Then why, I began, but he interrupted.

"We don't keep niggers," he said, "we don't want social equality."

Neither do I, I replied gently, I want a bed.

I walked thoughtfully to the train. I'll take a sleeper through Texas. I'm a bit dissatisfied with this town.

"Can't sell you one."

I only want to hire it, said I, for a couple of nights.

"Can't sell you a sleeper in Texas," he maintained. "They consider that social equality."

I consider it barbarism, I said, and I think I'll walk.

Walking, I met a wayfarer who immediately walked to the other side of the road where it was muddy. I asked his reasons.

"Niggers is dirty," he said.

So is mud, said I. Moreover I added, I am not as dirty as you—at least not yet.

"But you're a nigger, ain't you?" he asked.

My grandfather was so called.

"Well then!" he answered triumphantly.

Do you live in the South? I persisted, pleasantly.

"Sure," he growled, "and starve there."

I should think you and the Negroes might get together and vote out starvation.

"We don't let them vote."

We? Why not? I said in surprise.

"Niggers is too ignorant to vote."

But, I said, I am not so ignorant as you.

"But you're a nigger."

Yes, I'm certainly what you mean by that.

"Well then!" he returned, with that curiously inconsequential note of triumph. "Moreover," he said, "I don't want my sister to marry a nigger."

I had not seen his sister, so I merely murmured, let her say no.

"By God you shan't marry her, even if she said yes."

But—but I don't want to marry her, I answered, a little perturbed at the personal turn.

"Why not?" he yelled, angrier than ever.

Because I'm already married and I rather like my wife.

"Is she a nigger?" he asked suspiciously.

Well, I said again, her grandmother—was called that.

"Well then!" he shouted in that oddly illogical way.

I gave up.

Go on, I said, either you are crazy or I am.

"We both are," he said as he trotted along in the mud.

From *The Crisis*, 1922.

It must have taken a special *genius for cruelty to devise the Jim Crow system. It was de-signed not only to "separate the races," but to humiliate and torture the Negro. Discrimination in public accommodations would seem to have been forbidden under the Fourteenth Amendment to the Constitution. Adopted in 1868, it said Ne-groes were citizens entitled to equal treatment under the law. But racial separation went on, and spread to more and more of man's everyday activities. In the 1920s, 14 states had Jim Crow laws for railroad travel. The laws said that accommoda-tions for both races should be "equal in all points of service and convenience." That was only lip service to the Supreme*

Court's "separate but equal" ruling of 1896. No one expected railroads to spend the money needed to give the nonvoting black minority the same facilities offered the white. It was not until the 1960s that new Civil Rights Acts outlawed segregation in transportation as well as other public accommodations. And even now, unless officials enforce the law, it can mean little in practice.

The account of a Jim Crow journey that follows was written in 1922 by William Pickens, then a field secretary of the National Association for the Advancement of Colored People. His parents were ex-slaves who became sharecroppers. For much of his childhood Pickens lived in semipeonage. But finally, defying the protest of the plantation boss, he began his schooling near Little Rock. He got up at four every morning, worked a half-day in the fields before school began, then went back to the fields after classes ended. There must have been—there still are—tens of thousands of other Negro boys whose promise is choked off by the harshness and poverty of life on the plantations. William Pickens, one of the few who escaped, earned scholarships for four years at Yale, and graduated with Phi Beta Kappa honors. He became a lecturer and teacher until the new NAACP drew him into using his talents to advance the protest movement.

A trip
through Texas . . .
1923

. . . I SIT IN a Jim Crow car as I
write, between El Paso and San Antonio, Texas. . . . In Al-
buquerque I had bought my reservation to El Paso, Texas. El
Paso is where the train would enter Texas, and my ticket ter-
minated there. But so thoroughly is it understood that Jim
Crowism is not designed merely to "separate," but also to
humiliate, colored passengers that the thing is always in the
consciousness of the railway employees, even those who oper-
ate in and out of Jim Crow territory, and they begin to "work
on you" as soon as you buy a ticket that leads even to the
limbo of this hell.

"Well, you can't ride in this car after you get into Texas.
You'll have to get out of this car in Texas, and I suppose you
know that?" This from the Pullman conductor, in a very gruff
and loud voice, so that the whole car might hear him, while
he and others stare and glare upon me. His speech is absolutely
unnecessary since my tickets call only for El Paso, but the

object is to "rub it in." I answered with not a word nor a look, save such mild and indifferent observations as I might bestow upon idiots who should spit at me or lick out their tongues as I passed by their cells of confinement.

In El Paso, because of the miscarriage of a telegram, my friends did not meet the train and I had to call them up and wait till they came down. I was meanwhile shown to the Negro waiting-room, a space of about twenty by twenty, away off in one corner of the station structure like a place of quarantine or a veritable hole in the wall. I had to traverse the entire length of the great main waiting-room in order to reach this hole. This main waiting-room has all the conveniences, 'phone booths, ticket offices, and what not. And whom do you suppose I saw in this main waiting-room as I passed through? Not only the "white people," but all the non-American "colored peoples," yellow Chinese, brown Japanese, and the many-colored Mexicans. . . . When I reached the little humiliating hole assigned to "Negroes," I found there only four or five colored people, all intelligent, not one of them conspicuously unkempt like some of the Mexicans in the main waiting-room. Those Mexicans were being treated as human beings, as they should be treated. These colored people knew that this arrangement was not so much for their separation as for their humiliation and attemped degradation, and it formed the burden of their conversation.

I stayed in El Paso two nights and three days. Its colored people are alert to the situation. By means of their automobiles they protected me against the "rear-seat" treatment of the electric street cars. They took me across the shallow Rio Grande into Mexico, just a few hundred yards from Jim Crowism. And over there, bless you, white and black people come out of Texas and gamble at the same table, drink at the same bar, and eat in the same restaurant, while the dark and almost black Mexican stands around as the policeman and the law.

Then I went to buy a ticket for San Antonio. I did not expect to buy a Pullman ticket, but I did expect to buy a day coach ticket on any train. But I found that colored passengers are allowed to go to San Antonio on but one train a day, and one that leaves at night. The morning train carried only Pullmans, and colored folk are made to wait twelve hours longer for the train that carries a Jim Crow compartment. A colored man's mother may be dying in San Antonio, but he must wait. Any Mexican . . . can ride on any train. Any foreigner . . . can travel freely, but not the mothers or wives or sisters of the black Americans who fought, bled, and died in France. All the rest of the world, be he an unlettered Mexican peon, an untrammeled Indian, or a representative of the uncivilized "white trash" of the South, can get either train; but the Negro, be he graduate of Harvard or bishop of the church, can go only once daily. Now if the Negro can be limited to once a day while others ride on any train, the Negro can be limited to one day a week while others ride seven, or even to one day a month while others ride thirty.

I took the train that leaves at night. It is a ride of about twenty-four hours. Through friends it had been arranged that I be given a berth, late at night, after all the white people had gone to sleep and could not see me, and perhaps be called early before any of the whites were up. The money was accepted from my friends, even tips, but only the porter was sent to bring me a pillow into the Jim Crow car, and they still have the money. In the morning I went back to see if I could get some breakfast in the dining car, before 7 o'clock, before the whites got hungry. And what did I find as I passed through the whole string of Pullman cars in the rear? All the races of the world, as usual, save only the most loyal of all Americans.

In the Jim Crow car there was but one toilet and washroom for use of colored women and men. And the Jim Crow car is not a car, mind you, but only the end of a car, part of the white men's smoker, separated from the white smokers only by a partition that rises part of the way from the floor toward the ceiling, so that all the sickening smoke can drift over all night and all day. . . .

When I reached the dining-car there was not another person there. I was asked did I "want anything." I replied briefly, breakfast. Then there was confusion and much conferring between the steward and several colored waiters at the other end of the car. The steward kept glancing at me meanwhile, as if endeavoring to "size me." Finally I was given a seat at the end of the car where the porters eat. Oatmeal, eggs, and postum were brought, and then a green curtain was drawn between me and the rest of the vacant dining-car! Remember, this did not all happen in some insane asylum, but in Texas. The check on which I was to order my food was a green check, a "porter's check," so that I should not need to be treated to such little formalities as an extra plate or a finger bowl. I deliberately wrote my name down in the blank for "porter," but I was charged a passenger's fare. It all meant that I would not eat any more that day, although I was not to reach San Antonio till eight or nine at night.

One must be an idiot not to comprehend the meaning and

the aim of these arrangements. There is no such thing as a fair and just Jim Crow system with "equal accommodations," and in very human nature there will never be. The inspiration of Jim Crow is a feeling of caste and a desire to "keep in its place," that is, to degrade, the weaker group. For there is no more reason for a Jim Crow car in public travel than there would be for a Jim Crow path in the public streets. Those honest-souled, innocent-minded people who do not know, but who think that the Jim Crow system of the South is a bona fide effort to preserve mere racial integrity on a plane of justice are grievously misled. Any man should be permitted to shut out whom he desires from his private preserves, but justice and Jim Crowism in public places and institutions are as far apart and as impossible of union as God and Mammon.

From *The Nation,* August 15, 1923.

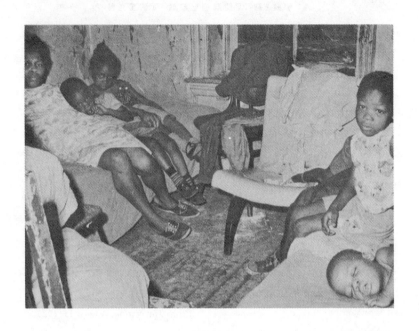

"I am huntin' for a city, to stay awhile," ran one of the old songs Negroes sang before the Civil War. They might have been dreaming of free Canaan's shore. In the twenties Negroes arriving in Chicago or Cleveland from the country had great trouble finding room to sit down in the new Canaan. All but a few corners of the cities were closed to them. The only housing they could find was in rundown and packed black ghettoes. By 1912 Louisville had put the first housing segregation law on the books. If a block had a majority of whites it was labeled for whites only, and vice versa. One after another cities followed the pattern and soon ghettoes were legally sanctioned in many parts of the country.

Even when Negroes of the professional or business class had the income to support homes in attractive and quiet neighborhoods it was very hard to find sellers. Such neighborhoods were almost always all white and did not welcome Negroes. If sales did occur (at prices that went through the ceiling), disaster often followed for the Negro family.

Take the case of Dr. Ossian Sweet. The Negro physician bought a home in a white neighborhood of Detroit in 1925. Not peace and quiet came, but hatred and headlines. Dr. Sweet's family was besieged by a mob; in self-defense his younger brother Henry fired back, and one of the attackers fell dead. The Sweet family and their friends in the house at the time were all arrested and charged with willful murder. The NAACP took up the cause, securing the great lawyer, Clarence Darrow, to defend them.

In The Crisis, Dr. DuBois discussed the issue of the Negro's right to his home and his right to defend it. The press gave the case great publicity. In his closing speech to the jury, Darrow exposed the race prejudice behind the trial by pointing out that if white men had killed a Negro while protecting their family and home from a mob of blacks, "no one would have dreamed of having them indicted. . . . They would have been given medals instead."

The jury of 12 white men brought in a verdict of "Not guilty." A precedent had been set in the law. A man's home was his castle, even if he was a Negro.

What would you do?

1925

IN DETROIT, MICHIGAN, a black man has shot into a mob which was threatening him, his family, his friends, and his home in order to make him move out of the neighborhood. He killed one man and wounded another.

Immediately a red and awful challenge confronts the nation. Must black folk shoot and shoot to kill in order to maintain their rights or is this unnecessary and wanton bloodshed for fancied ill? The answer depends on the facts. The Mayor of Detroit has publicly warned both mob and Negroes. He has repudiated mob law but he adds, turning to his darker audience, that they ought not to invite aggression by going where they are not wanted. There are thus two interpretations:

1. A prosperous Negro physician of Detroit, seeking to get away from his people, moves into a white residential section where his presence for social reasons is distasteful to his neighbors.

2. A prosperous Negro physician of Detroit, seeking a bet-

ter home with more light, air, space and quiet, finds it naturally in the parts of the city where white folk with similar wants have gone rather than in the slums where most of the colored are crowded.

Which version is true? See the figures:

NEGRO POPULATION OF DETROIT

1900 . . 4,111
1910 . . 5,741
1920 . . 40,838
1925 . . 60,000 (estimated)

Two thirds of this population in 1920 were crowded into three wards—the Third, Fifth and Seventh. Meantime the total population of Detroit has more than doubled in ten years and the people have reached out on all sides to new dwelling places. Have the Negroes no right to reach too? Is it not their duty to seek better homes and, if they do, are they not bound to "move into white neighborhoods" which is simply another way of saying "move out of congested slums"?

Why do they not make their own new settlements then? Because no individual can make a modern real estate development; no group of ordinary individuals can compete with organized real estate interests and get a decent deal. When Negroes have tried it they have usually had miserable results . . . In Macon, Savannah, New Orleans and Atlanta crime and prostitution have been kept and protected in Negro residence districts. In New York City, for years, no Negro could rent or buy a home in Manhattan outside the "Tenderloin"; and white Religion and Respectability, far from stretching a helping hand, turned and cursed the blacks when by bribery, politics and brute force they broke into the light and air of Harlem. . . .

Dear God! Must we not live? And if we live may we not live somewhere? And when a whole city full of white folk led and helped by banks, Chambers of Commerce, mortgage companies and "realtors" are combing the earth for every decent bit of residential property for whites, where in the name of God can we live and live decently if not by these same whites? If some of the horror-struck and law-worshipping white leaders of Detroit instead of winking at the Ku Klux Klan and admonishing the Negroes to allow themselves to be kicked and killed with impunity—if these would finance and administer a decent scheme of housing relief for Negroes it would not be necessary for us to kill white mob leaders in order to live in peace and decency. These whited sepulchres pulled that trigger and not the man that held the gun.

But, wail the idiots, Negroes depress real estate values! This is a lie—an ancient and bearded lie. Race prejudice decreases values both real estate and human; crime, ignorance and filth decrease values. But a decent, quiet, educated family buying property in a decent neighborhood will not affect values a bit unless the people in that neighborhood hate a colored skin more than they regard the value of their own property. This has been proven in a thousand instances. Sudden fall in values comes through propaganda and hysteria manipulated by real estate agents, or by Southern slave drivers who want their labor to return South, or by ignorant gossip mongers. Usually Negroes do not move into new developments but into districts which well-to-do whites are deserting. The fall in values is not due to race but to a series of economic readjustments and often, as in Baltimore, real estate values were actually saved and raised, not lowered when black folk bought Druid Hill Avenue and adjacent streets. Certainly a flood of noisy dirty black folk will ruin any neighborhood but they ruin black property as well as white, and the reason is not their color but their condition. And whom, High Heaven, shall we blame for that?

From *The Crisis,* November, 1925.

"LET THE VOICE OF BESSIE SMITH
PENETRATE THE CLOSED EARS. . . ."

There was a direct connection between the militancy of men like Dr. Ossian Sweet—who took up arms to defend his home from a mob—and the New Negro movement in the arts. The younger writers published in Alain Locke's anthology The New Negro had turned their backs on Booker T. Washington. They did not want to "accommodate" or "adjust." With W. E. B. DuBois, they stood for full equality. Many of these younger writers were the sons of the rising middle class. But they were not dedicated to making money or to imitating the white folks. Nor did they want to separate themselves from the black masses. They looked for and found enduring values in their own people, in their folkways, in their work and play, in their heart and spirit.

In 1926 one of the leading young writers, Langston Hughes (then 24), published an article calling on Negro artists to look closely at the life around them and write it and paint it as it was. Don't be like the Negro society woman who pays for a front row seat at a concert of European folk songs, he said, but who wouldn't think of going to hear a Negro blues singer. His statement was an historic declaration of independence for the Negro artist.

Free within ourselves . . .

1926

. . . THE ROAD FOR the serious black artist who would produce a racial art is most certainly rocky and the mountain is high. Until recently he received almost no encouragement for his work from either white or colored people. The fine novels of Chesnutt go out of print with neither race noticing their passing. The quaint charm and humor of Dunbar's dialect verse brought to him, in his day, largely the same kind of encouragement one would give a side-show freak (A colored man writing poetry! How odd!), a clown (How amusing!).

The present vogue in things Negro, although it may do as much harm as good for the budding colored artist, has at least done this: it has brought him forcibly to the attention of his own people among whom for so long, unless the other race had noticed him beforehand, he was a prophet with little honor. . . .

The Negro artist works against an undertow of sharp criticism and misunderstanding from his own group and unintentional bribes from the whites. "O, be respectable, write about nice people, show how good we are," say the Negroes. "Be stereotyped, don't go too far, don't shatter our illusions about you, don't amuse us too seriously. We will pay you," say the whites. . . .

But in spite of the Nordicized Negro intelligentsia and the desires of some white editors we have an honest American Negro literature already with us. Now I await the rise of the Negro theater. Our folk music, having achieved world-wide fame, offers itself to the genius of the great individual American Negro composer who is to come. And within the next decade I expect to see the work of a growing school of colored artists who paint and model the beauty of dark faces and create with new technique the expressions of their own soul-world. And the Negro dancers who will dance like flame and the singers who will continue to carry our songs to all who listen— they will be with us in even greater numbers tomorrow.

Most of my own poems are racial in theme and treatment, derived from the life I know. In many of them I try to grasp and hold some of the meanings and rhythms of jazz. I am sincere as I know how to be in these poems and yet after every reading I answer questions like these from my own people: Do you think Negroes should always write about Negroes? I wish you wouldn't read some of your poems to white folks. How do you find anything interesting in a place like a cabaret? Why do you write about black people? You aren't black. What makes you do so many jazz poems?

But jazz to me is one of the inherent expressions of Negro life in America: the eternal tom-tom beating in the Negro soul

—the tom-tom of revolt against weariness in a white world, a world of subway trains, and work, work, work; the tom-tom of joy and laughter, and pain swallowed in a smile. Yet the Philadelphia clubwoman is ashamed to say that her race created it and she does not like me to write about it. The old subconscious "white is best" runs through her mind. Years of study under white teachers, a lifetime of white books, pictures, and papers, and white manners, morals, and Puritan standards made her dislike the spirituals. And now she turns up her nose at jazz and all its manifestations—likewise almost everything else distinctly racial. . . . She does not want a true picture of herself from anybody. She wants the artist to flatter her, to make the white world believe that all Negroes are as smug and as near white in soul as she wants to be. But, to my mind, it is the duty of the younger Negro artist, if he accepts any duties at all from outsiders, to change through the force of his art that old whispering "I want to be white," hidden in the aspirations of his people, to "Why should I want to be white? I am a Negro—and beautiful!"

So I am ashamed for the black poet who says, "I want to be a poet, not a Negro poet," as though his own racial world were not as interesting as any other world. I am ashamed, too, for the colored artist who runs from the painting of Negro faces to the painting of sunsets after the manner of the academicians because he fears the strange un-whiteness of his own features. An artist must be free to choose what he does, certainly, but he must also never be afraid to do what he might choose.

Let the blare of Negro jazz bands and the bellowing voice of Bessie Smith singing blues penetrate the closed ears of the colored near-intellectuals until they listen and perhaps understand. Let Paul Robeson singing *Water Boy,* and Rudolph Fisher writing about the streets of Harlem, and Jean Toomer holding the heart of Georgia in his hands, and Aaron Douglas drawing strange black fantasies cause the smug Negro middle class to turn from their white, respectable, ordinary books and papers to catch a glimmer of their own beauty. We younger Negro artists who create now intend to express our individual dark-skinned selves without fear or shame. If white people are pleased we are glad. If they are not, it doesn't matter. We know we are beautiful. And ugly too. The tom-tom cries and the tom-tom laughs. If colored people are pleased we are glad. If they are not, their displeasure doesn't matter either. We build our temples for tomorrow, strong as we know how, and we stand on top of the mountain, free within ourselves.

From *The Nation,* June 23, 1926.

Harlem's Negroes numbered 50,000 on the eve of World War I. By 1920 black Harlem stretched from 130th Street to 145th and from Madison to Eighth Avenue and included 80,000 people. Ten years later the southern border had moved down to 110th Street and the Negro population had swelled to 200,000. (Indeed, by 1940 there were 11 cities with as many as 100,000 Negroes.) Loften Mitchell, author of many plays and essays, provides this personal memoir of what it was like to grow up in Harlem in the thirties.

This is me!
I'm somebody!...

1930s

THE SMALL TOWN of black Harlem, though surrounded by hostility, was crowded with togetherness, love, human warmth, and neighborliness. Southern Negroes fled from physical lynchings and West Indians from economic lynchings. They met in the land north of 110th Street and they brought with them their speech patterns, folkways, mores, and their dogged determination. They brought, too, their religiosity and their gregariousness and they created here a distinct nation that was much like a small town. Readily welcomed were newly arrived relatives and strangers, and these were maintained until they found jobs and homes. In this climate everyone knew everyone else. A youngster's misbehavior in any house earned him a beating there plus one when he got home. In this climate the cooking of chitterlings brought a curious neighbor to the door: "Mrs. Mitchell, you cooking chitterlings? I thought you might need a little cornbread to go with 'em." A moment later a West Indian neighbor appeared

75

with rice and beans. Another neighbor followed with some beer to wash down the meal. What started as a family supper developed into a building party.

This climate created in Harlem a human being with distinct characteristics. The child of Harlem had the will to survive, to "make it." He was taught, "If you're going to be a bum, be the best bum." He was taught, too, a burning distrust for whites, to strike them before they struck, that to "turn the other cheek" was theologically correct, but physically incorrect in dealing with white folks. He learned to hold out his right hand, but to clench his left hand if the "flesh wasn't pinched in a decent handshake." This Harlem child learned to laugh in the face of adversity, to cry in the midst of plentifulness, to fight quickly and reconcile easily. He became a "backcapping" signifying slicker and a suave, sentimental gentleman. From his African, Southern Negro and West Indian heritage, he knew the value of gregariousness and he held group consultations on the street corners to review problems of race, economics, or politics.

He was poor, but proud. He hid his impoverishment with clothes, pseudo-good living, or sheer laughter. Though he complained of being broke, he never admitted his family was poor. "My old man puts all his dough in the bank," was the common complaint. "That's why I'm out here, stashed like a tramp." When the Harlemite stood on breadlines, he had a glib statement: "I'm here, picking up some food for some poor old lady next door to me." If he were seen in the relief office, he let you know he was there trying to get a poor neighbor on relief. This Harlem child had to have something—a car, a sharp wit, sharp clothing, a ready laugh, a loud voice, a beautiful woman. He had the burning need to belong to something, own something, and let the world know: "This is me! I'm somebody!"

I know. I felt it. We had to have that will to survive, for bloody street fighting bruised our bodies and a sadistic school system attempted to destroy our hearts and minds. Sadism was —in the 1920's and 1930's—a pre-requisite for teaching in the public schools. Incompetent, inept teachers sought "butts" for bad jokes. Knowledge-hungry black children were excellent targets. These teachers knew nothing and cared little about Negroes and wondered why they had to put up with them. Since neither teacher nor pupil had been exposed to Negro history, the black child sat in class, unwanted, barely tolerated. . . .

Harlem life was difficult, but it was fun. In the nineteen-thirties we had our own language, sung openly, defiantly. We resorted to it like other groups when we wanted to exclude people. We loved to see the puzzled white faces when one Negro asked: "What you putting down?" The answer was: "I'm putting down all skunks, punks, and a hard hustle!" If someone "backcapped" you, you might tell him: "We ain't cousins, so we can sure play dozens! And you know we ain't brothers, so we can sure talk about mothers!' An inquiry regarding one's welfare brought this response: "I'm like the bear, I ain't nowhere. I'm like the bear's brother. I ain't gon' get no further." If someone expressed disbelief, he was told: "If I'm lying, I'm flying. In fact, Jack, if I'm lying, God's gone to Jackson, Mississippi, and you know He wouldn't be hanging out down there!" There were other expressions, too: To be "beat to your sox" was to be penniless. To be "sent" was to be in a heavenly state and if something "sent your brown body," you were in orbit! If you were "taking charge," you were in command of a situation and "coming on like Gang Busters." But, if you were a "lane from Spain," you were "dead out of the country —from Blip, which is down south where if you ain't white, it's a Blip—or from South America, that foreign country known as Alabama, Georgia, or Mississippi." You had to be "hip as a whip, have your boots laced, or else you were a crumb, subject to be swept out of a place!" If your "boots were laced," you made it to the Apollo Theatre each and every Friday. The new show started then. Every Harlemite and his brother showed, defying all truant officers. You had to "fall" into the second balcony, see someone you knew on the other side of the place, then yell: "Hey, there, Daddy-O!" The fellow on the other side—who had been sitting there, praying he would see an acquaintance—returned your greeting in loud, friendly tones: "Man! I ain't seen you in a month of Sundays! How's every little thing?" "Jumping!" you answered. "Pick you up on the rebound!"

Fortified and recognized, you sat down. Luis Russell, Jimmy Lunceford, Teddy Hill, Lucky Millinder—or whatever band played that week—started swinging the Apollo theme song. You had to show the chick next to you that you knew the words: "I think you're wonderful. I may be wrong. I think you're wonderful. I think you're swell!" And, of course, if you could get the next line, you really rated: "Your smiling face and shining eyes—"

By the end of the first number you were either "spieling" to the chick next to you, or you had struck up an acquaintance with someone close to you. As the music played, you stomped your feet and the whole balcony rocked.

Pigmeat Markham, George Wiltshire, Johnny Lee Long, Johnny Hudgins, Eddie Green, Eddie Hunter, Ralph Cooper, Jimmy Baskette and Dusty Fletcher fed us a thousand laughs. We roared at our economic plight, our race problem, and at life itself. One skit during the height of the depression indicated our willingness to laugh at our economic plight: The lights came up on Pigmeat and Ralph Cooper, strolling on stage, counting rolls of bills they held: "Twenty. Forty. Sixty," they counted in unison. Suddenly Pigmeat froze, then exploded, angrily: "What the hell is this one dollar bill doing here?" He ripped the bill into shreds. Ralph Cooper admonished him: "Man! As long as you hang out with me, don't you ever be caught with a damn one dollar bill!"

But, it was Sunday afternoon in Harlem that offered the week's most exciting times. Seventh Avenue, then a fashionable tree-lined, swank boulevard, was kept immaculate by community pride and by city authorities who fined building superintendents two dollars for allowing rubbish on sidewalks. No one dared to be caught dressed sloppily on Seventh Avenue —colored folks' Broadway. Residents would stare at you, and then you got a long lecture at home about "shaming" the family name. Besides, the existence of Negro policemen—Brisbane, Brown, Pendleton, and Lacey—assured the community that Seventh Avenue would remain impeccable and orderly. Seventh Avenue on Sunday afternoon was where you strolled. No one who knew Harlem from the nineteen-twenties through the nineteen-forties can forget "strolling." We youngsters had suits issued by the WPA (Works Progress Administration). We had tailors "drape" these, put on shirts and ties, wide snap-brimmed hats, then called on our young ladies.

Strolling, despite its seeming casualness, was exacting. It had a plan and a purpose. You had to walk with your right leg dipping a bit, resembling a limp. Your fedora was snapped smartly over your right eye. You and your young lady started just below 116th Street, moving north up Seventh Avenue. Three hours and a half after the start of your stroll, you made it to Henry's Sugar Bowl on 135th Street. There you had a malted and met other friends. Then—you started "strolling" downtown. You told the world: "This is black me, in my Harlem. I belong here and I'm somebody!"

Man, we strolled!

We celebrated, too—for any and every reason. The first solo flight to Paris caused a dance to be named the "Lindy Hop." We stood on street corners and cried when Florence Mills died and we sang *Memories of You* with profound respect. We listened, eagerly, to Jack Johnson or any other Negro who had beaten the "system" as he reported to us from the Lincoln Theatre stage. And we loved the New York Yankees. They were our ball club. . . .

Our biggest celebrations were on nights when Joe Louis fought. The Brown Bomber, appearing in the darkness when Italy invaded Ethiopia and the Scottsboro Boys faced lynching, became a black hero the history books could not ignore. It is for sociologists and psychologists to define what Joe meant to Negroes. Writers certainly have failed to do it. But, he was there, and I knew he was there, and he knew I was there. When he won a fight I went into the streets with other Negroes and I hollered until I was hoarse. Then, Joe would come to Harlem, to the Theresa, and he couldn't say what he felt when he saw us hollering at him. And he didn't have to. To paraphrase that old Negro expression: He didn't have to say a mumbling word!

We had culture, too. The Schomburg Collection, a mighty fortress, fed us materials withheld from white history books. Three theatres—the Lincoln, Lafayette, and the Alhambra—housed stock companies, then later became movie and vaudeville houses. In these houses Louis Armstrong's trumpet blared, defiantly, at the world. Cab Calloway hi-de-hoed, Bill "Bojangles" Robinson tap-danced up staircases, and Bessie Smith sang the blues from the soul of a black woman. Here, too, Langston Hughes, Countee Cullen, Arna Bontemps, and others wrote magnificent lines about us. Romare Bearden, Charles Alston, Ernest Crichlow, Charles White, Augusta Savage, and Jacob Lawrence created wonderful works of art about me. The *Amsterdam News* and the *Courier* and the *Age* and the *People's Voice* roared for me.

Much of this Harlem exists today. Interested television and movie cameras, journalists and writers can find numerous art centers, galleries, writers, painters, sculptors, and other cultural forces thriving here. And they could find people, real people, alive, aware. But, a hostile white world is unwilling to see all of Harlem. The community's false friends paint it a jungle or slum, a land of dark terror where "beasts" are created. This is the voice that, allied with other virulent forces, cannot afford to recognize Harlem's humanity and that of black people. Much of the anxiety of modern times has been created because white America has been unable and unwilling to recognize Negroes as people on any basis.

The first generation Harlemites, now past sixty, remain here. Their children—denied the opportunity of buying homes in

Harlem by the Mortgage Conference—live in far-flung places. The absentee landlord owns the area and he is not interested in clean streets nor in pressuring indifferent city authorities to enforce health regulations. Newly arrived southerners live beside the first generation Harlemites. These newcomers may be attempting to adjust to urban life, but their children are impatient, angry. They see this violent land of church bombings, firehoses, crooked politicians and policemen, Indian-killers and home-run hitters. They see recklessness and lawlessness in a time when man can hit the moon, but fail to claim his identity here in this large world. . . .

From *Freedomways,* Fall, 1964.

Newspapers play a big part in
shaping the ideas of most people. (Before the days of movies,
radio, and television, it was an even bigger part.) The fight for
fair treatment of news about Negroes has an ancient history.
All too often, if the news was good, the press omitted it; if it
was bad, it was played up and slanted to build a picture of the
criminal Negro. An intensive study of a dozen major newspapers, North and South, made by the historian Rayford W.
Logan, has shown how negative was the picture drawn of the
Negro at the turn of the century. (That was some time ago,
but the newspapers changed only slowly, and some are still
doing it.) "Burly negro," "negro ruffian," "African Annie,"

8 3

"colored cannibal" were terms used in the news stories, and in the jokes and cartoons "coon," "darky," "pickaninny," and "nigger" were commonplace. Even the leading literary magazines of that day, edited for polite and educated society—Harper's, Century, Atlantic Monthly—*regularly used derisive terms in their stories, cartoons, poems, and articles.*

The effect was to make the reader take for granted that the Negro was stupid, lazy, immoral, a clown, a liar, a thief, a drunkard.

The word "Negro" was not capitalized by any newspaper until the Boston Transcript *did it in 1900. The move had little influence on others. Then, in 1920, Marcus Garvey's nationalist movement, the Universal Negro Improvement Association, demanded in convention that the word "Negro" be spelled with a capital "N" in accord with the new Negro's self-respect. The campaign began to take hold, and in 1929 the state board of education ordered all New York schools to teach the spelling of "Negro" with a capital "N." The next year* The New York Times, *the country's most powerful newspaper, announced it would capitalize the word.* Opportunity, *the voice of the Urban League, noted the change in policy and commented on what it ought to lead to.*

With a capital "N" . . .

1930

IN AN EDITORIAL ANENT its decision to capitalize hereafter the "N" in the word Negro when it appears in its columns, *The New York Times* of a recent date says:

"*The New York Times* now joins many of the leading Southern newspapers as well as most of the Northern in according this recognition. In our 'style book' 'Negro' is now added to the list of words to be capitalized. It is not merely a typographical change; it is an act in recognition of racial self-respect for those who have been for generations 'in the lower case.' "

This is a fine sentiment and when powerful newspapers such as the *Times* and *Sun* and such magazines as the conservative *Atlantic Monthly* and the popular *Saturday Evening Post* depart voluntarily from typographical usage which had its genesis in the social disabilities transmitted by the regime of slavery, it is evidence beyond dispute that a new evaluation of the Negro is under way.

Such a new evaluation can be infinitely hastened or indefinitely postponed by the attitude of the press. To a great degree the composite Negro, the popular "stereotype," is the creation of newspapers and magazines which have persistently kept alive the Negro of fancy, of myth, of the ante-bellum and reconstruction period. It might not be too much to say, even, that not a little of the prejudice which the Negro is called upon to overcome is stimulated by the method of treatment of news involving Negroes, especially when a Negro is suspected of a criminal act. The practice of designating the racial origin of the perpetrator of crime, when he is a Negro, has done the Negro race untold harm. This practice is inexcusable and would be universally condemned if applied consistently to all nationalities and races.

The next step, then, in lifting the Negro out of the lower case demands a change in the method of treating Negroes in the news columns. It should not be a difficult one to take, since the only requirement is that he should be treated as other Americans.

From Opportunity, April, 1930.

T*he crash of the stock market in 1929 signaled the coming of the Great Depression. But for most Negroes hard times were just like old times. Since slavery, poverty had been general on the Southern countryside. Farm laborer and sharecropper never made a decent living. Early in the twenties soil erosion, the boll weevil, and foreign competition in cotton turned bad living into worse. The gay times of the years of the Charleston craze were unknown in farm cabins.*

Nor were boom times universally enjoyed in the city tenements. American prosperity was not something parcelled out equally to all. Those working in the shipyards, in the coal fields, in the shoe and textile mills were scraping along. As the first flutters of alarm were felt even before the crash of '29, thousands of Negroes were laid off. When disaster became widespread, with businesses collapsing and banks failing, proportionately more black workers than white lost their jobs. In 1931, about one out of three Negroes was jobless, and one out of four whites.

With little or no savings to fall back on, what would happen to the unemployed? It was the Urban League's job to find out. In 1931, while the depression was still shooting down to greater depths, out of New York and Pittsburgh came these firsthand reports of the hardships Negroes were facing.

Just hanging on . . .

1931

NEW YORK

. . . THE R. FAMILY CAME to New York thirty years ago. Eddie, the oldest son, who is twenty-three, was employed in a paint and supply store up to June, when he was laid off. Margaret, age twenty, lost her job in a hat factory that closed down in September. Two children are in high school and two in elementary school. The rent, $65 per month, is four months in arrears, with eviction threatened. When visited the children had been out of school, as they were without shoes and suitable clothing.

The Fords have seven children and expect another in March. Since eviction in October they have occupied one room in a cold water flat, depending wholly on the generosity of neighbors for support. When visited they were without food or fuel. Mr. F. wept like a child when he told the visitor that Mrs. Ford with the baby was at a neighbor's house to keep warm. The entire family invariably slept with their clothes on as there was little or no bedding. Newspapers were frequently placed over the children at night. Two of the children have been given away and the rest have been "farmed" out to neighbors.

T. J. had resolved to "end the whole damned business." And so when he arrived at the investigator's desk, it wasn't a job he wanted, but a loan of fifty cents. With difficulty the interviewer drew out of him that this was to be spent for a bottle of bi-chloride of mercury. Finally, after being supplied with clothing and a job, a clipping was revealed which gave account of a suicide on the preceding day, the victim being the applicant's room-mate who, being out of work for ten months and in despondency, had dressed himself in his evening suit, leaving a note saying, "Death can't be any worse than what I have suffered."

But the silent sufferers who, like the Aspinards from Louisiana, are "too proud to beg," never find their way into a relief agency. Shivering about an oil stove, with five children sick, they had never accepted charity and had never heard of the relief agencies.

Faith may remove mountains, but it is still "the substance of things hoped for," at least in so far as job seeking goes in the Jenks family. J. has lived with his wife and six children, paying $62 per month rent until May, 1929, when he lost his regular job. The family lived for fourteen years at the same address. When they moved to the present basement, the radio and other furniture were forfeited for back rent. Mr. J., thrifty and righteous, had a substantial savings account which has now been used up. Insurance policies have lapsed. Being a "God fearing" man, he finds it hard to explain his present predicament, having always been taught at church to which he has been a regular contributor, to "trust in the Lord." He is still praying that he may yet find a job.

G. S., now twenty-two, left college at the age of nineteen because his father was ill, and there being five smaller children, he became the main support. Since coming from Georgia ten years ago, with the mother working, they had saved about $2,000 which was invested in a suburban home in Jamaica, but unemployment hit them almost a year ago. Foreclosure proceedings followed. Not being the "head of the family," he could not qualify for an emergency work job.

Hundreds of persons have during the past few months experienced similar hardships. From ten to twenty eviction cases per day are reported at the Urban League. Fully seventy-five percent of the persons applying for relief are unknown to relief agencies, and up to the past year have never before requested aid. Many have voluntarily given up their homes, pawned their clothes, sold their furniture and are persistently hanging on by the barest thread. . . .

PITTSBURGH

We visit the more or less temporary quarters provided by a group of socially-minded business men as a refuge for men rendered homeless by unemployment. There it stands, a broad, massive five-storied brick structure, overlooking the river. Inside, one feels immediately the impact of an impression of tragedy. . . .

Two thousand souls! Men casually referred to by the comfortably clothed, well-fed man as derelicts—flotsam and jetsam —bums—work dodgers. Two thousand men who roam the streets by day in search of work and return to this haven at night for a cup of stew or soup, and a "flop." White men and Negroes; swarthy Italians and Mexicans, stolid Poles, florid Irishmen and blond Swedes; milling about the spacious lobby of the great building. The newcomers among them distinguishable by their tatters and rags; one or two on crutches; many bearded and grimy, eyes bloodshot from loss of sleep or exposure to the unsympathetic elements. . . .

We manage to squeeze through the crowd that is assembled before the huge stage, the drabness of their existence being temporarily submerged by the flood of music being produced on the borrowed piano by a Negro player. We enter the combined kitchen and dining room which is the goal toward which is headed the almost endless queue of men which writhes and twists and doubles upon itself interminably. Our conductor pridefully points out his kitchen crew recruited from among his "guests." They are busy ladling out large tins of thick, potent soup which we found to be mighty palatable. But to see the eagerness with which the canisters are grasped, and the chunks of bread seized! Now and then comes the shrinking soul whose averted eyes and shamefaced expression immediately points him out as a new recruit to the army of unemployed; another scrap rejected by an impersonal industry; possibly a man reduced to the breadline who once looked upon charity as the refuge of only the indolent, the careless or the improvident. . . .

And everywhere are Negroes—at times seeming to represent the majority, but in reality constituting about forty percent of the two thousand men. Think of it. In a city where Negroes are but 8 percent of the total population, 40 percent are represented in this group of homeless, unemployed men.

But why so many Negroes? Consider Mr. Jones. He is now out of work, although for six years he has been employed by one concern which has not been greatly affected by the depression. "Why did you leave there?"

"I was just laid off—why? Because I wouldn't pay off the foreman. He knows us colored folks has to put up with everything to keep a job so he asks for two-three dollars anytime an' if you don't pay, you get a poor payin' job or a lay-off." Three fellow-workers support this testimony. "My division foreman charged me $20 one time for taking me back on, after he had laid me off; then asked me for $15 more after I had worked a while. I just got tired of that way of doin' and wouldn't pay him; now I'm out of a job."

And this statement is verified by the increasing number of calls from ambitious housewives who want "a bright, lively housemaid who can cook, do laundry and the regular housework, of course—and she must have the very best of references. How much will I pay? Well, there are so many people out of work that I am sure I can find a girl for $6 a week. Oh yes—and she must stay on the place as I have three children and we go out quite often."

To the desk of a colored worker in the city offices comes a middle-aged Negro woman, intense physical and mental suffering depicted on her face. She is the mother of six children, the oldest of whom is fifteen. She wants food to keep body and soul together, clothing to protect her brood from the chill winds; her gas is turned off because of overdue bills; she is threatened with eviction in five days if something is not done. "Where is your husband?" "He worked in the steel mills for four-five years and was a good man. The mill closed and he was laid off. He went out early every morning and walked the streets until night, looking for work. Day after day he done this ever since last June. Once a man told him that he needn't trouble looking for a job as long as there is so many white men out of work. I guess us colored folks don't get hungry like white folks. He just got discouraged and one day he went out and didn't come back. He told me once that if he wasn't living at home the welfare people would help me and the kids, and maybe he just went away on that account—and—maybe something has happened—" here tears gathered in the harassed eyes. . . .

Take the case of James Brown, who has been a sandblaster in one of the pipe mills for over eight years. Everyone who knows him says that he is honest, reliable and a valuable worker. He has four children who, for the first time in their lives are suffering the pangs of real, stark hunger. Yet his plea is not for food, fuel or clothing, but WORK which this highly organized and efficient society fails to provide. He is given a permit to sell apples on the city streets. . . .

From *Opportunity,* February and March, 1931.

N*ew York, Pittsburgh, Chicago . . . it was the same everywhere. In the "richest and greatest nation on earth" bank doors closed, farmers were forced off their land, millions were thrown out of work, cities were left without a dime to carry on government. And in those first and worst years of the depression, it was only the cities that made any attempt to provide public relief. Funds were low and ran out repeatedly. There was no help from the state governments; most of them did not even have welfare departments.*

In Washington President Hoover was saying that business conditions would get better by themselves. There was no need to do anything. He refused to permit federal funds to be spent on relief. Relief was the concern of the states and the communities, he said, or private charity.

In New York City families were given $2.39 a week to live on. In Detroit, allowances fell to fifteen cents a day per person and then ran out entirely. Only about one in four of the nation's unemployed could get relief. The pennies were allotted for food and fuel. If you needed shoes or a coat, a bed or medicine, you had to beg or steal them—or go without food to buy them.

But no one was starving, insisted President Hoover. He was wrong. The welfare figures showed they starved in the mountains of Kentucky and on the plains of Kansas. They starved in the cities and in the villages. And they died. Thousands of children died of the depression disease—not enough to eat.

Eviction became common when people had no money to pay the rent. Those kicked out moved in with relatives or friends when they could. The others roamed the streets or sought shelter in miserable, crowded municipal lodging houses. Hoovervilles—shacks made of castoff tin or boards—sprang up along riverbanks and railroad tracks or in vacant lots.

One day in 1931, in a restaurant on Chicago's South Side, Horace Cayton chanced to look up from his meal and saw through the window a long file of Negroes marching by three abreast. They seemed to be moving in a deadly earnest way to some invisible goal. He went outside and stepped into the ranks. What follows is his account of one of the many attempts to stop the eviction of a Negro family.

Cayton, a journalist and sociologist, was the grandson of Hiram Revels, one of the two Negroes who represented Mississippi in the United States Senate during Reconstruction.

No rent money . . .

1931

TURNING TO MY marching com-
panion I asked where we were headed for, and what we would
do when we got there. He looked surprised, and told me we
were marching down to put in a family who had been evicted
from a house for not paying their rent. Things were awfully
tough down in the Black Belt now, he continued, and jobs were
impossible to get. The Negro was the first to be discharged and
the last to be hired. Now with unemployment they were hungry, and if they were put out in the street their situation would
be a desperate one.

The Negroes of the community had been exploited for years
by the unscrupulous landlords who had taken advantage of
prejudice compelling the Negroes to live only in that district,
and had forced them to pay exorbitant rents. Now, continued
my informer, hard times had hit them and they were being
turned out into the street. Furthermore, as the Negroes did not
know their legal rights, the landlords would simply pitch their
few belongings out of the window with no legal procedure at
all. . . .

We finally came to a dirty, ill-kept street of houses. The first part of our line had arrived ahead, and had successfully put back into the house the few miserable belongings of the evicted tenants. The woman of the house was standing . . . intermittently crying and thanking God, loudly and dramatically. Her audience was very responsive, and seemed about to break into shouts itself. . . .

Suddenly a shout went around that there was another family in the next street that had been put out, and the procession started in that direction. This time I was far in the front to see the fun. We were met at the street by two squad cars of police who asked us where we were going. The black crowd swarmed around the officers and their cars like a hive of bees around their queen. The officers jumped out of their cars and told the crowd to move on. No one moved. Everyone simply stood and stared at them. One officer lost his head and drew his gun, leveling it at the crowd.

Then a young fellow stepped out of the crowd and said, "You can't shoot all of us and I might as well die now as any time. All we want is to see that these people, our people, get back into their homes. We have no money, no jobs, and sometimes no food. We've got to live some place. We are just acting the way you or anyone else would act."

The officer looked at the boy, at the crowd, and the crowd looked at him. No threats, no murmurs, no disorder; the crowd just looked at him. There the officer stood, surrounded by a crowd of dirty, ragged Negroes with a sea of black eyes on him. The officer replaced his gun in his holster and stood looking.

In the back of the crowd some one got up on a soap box and

started to speak. It was an old, wild-eyed hag-like woman. The crowd turned and listened to her. . . . This woman was not talking about any economic principles; she was not talking about any empty theories, nor was she concerned with some abstract utopia to be gained from the movement of the "lower classes." She was talking about bread, and jobs, and places to sleep in. It was the talk of a person who had awakened from a pleasant dream to find that reality was hard, cold, and cruel.

Then I realized that all these people had suddenly found themselves fact to face with hard, cold reality. They were the people who a few years ago had migrated from the South, in wagons, in cars, in trains, even walking. They had migrated with songs and hymns on their lips—with prayers to the Almighty for deliverance. They had come to the North and had been welcomed. Ah, America's great pool of unskilled labor was tapped; they had been sent to help win the war. But pretty soon the war was over. And, later still, the good times and prosperity were over. With hard times they had felt the pinch of poverty, and now they were virtually starving to death in the paradise of a few years ago.

The talk went on. The crowd stood and listened. It had grown bigger now and many white faces were seen. The officers stood and listened. I don't believe that there was any one there who was not touched by the talk. I don't believe that there was anybody there, white or black, who did not in some degree face the same situation that she was so vividly describing. Even the officers stood with more or less respectful attention. I spoke to one of the officers and asked if he didn't think it was a shame to put people out of their houses when they were in such desperate circumstances. He answered that it was tough, yet a man didn't build a house for charity—but it didn't make any difference to him as long as they started no trouble.

Just then a siren was heard—the whisper went around— the riot squad was coming!

All of the spectators stepped back, and the active partici- pants formed a small nucleus around the speaker—packed in tight—a solid black lump of people. Two young fellows stood holding the woman up on the soap box in the middle.

Then the riot squad turned into the street, four cars full of blue-coated officers and a patrol wagon. They jumped out be- fore the cars came to a stop and charged down upon the crowd. Night sticks and "billies" played a tattoo on black heads.

"Hold your places!" shouted the woman.

"Act like men!" answered the crowd.

They stood like dumb beasts—no one ran, no one fought or offered resistance, just stood, an immovable black mass. Finally the officers were through, and started to pull down the woman speaker. Clubs came down in a sickening rain of blows on the head of one of the boys who was holding her up. Blood spurted from his mouth and nose. Finally she was pulled down. A tremor of nervousness ran through the crowd. Then some- one turned and ran. In a minute the whole group was running like mad for cover. One of the officers shot twice at one of the boys who had been holding up the woman speaker. The boy stumbled, grabbed his thigh, but kept on running. The woman was struggling in the arms of two husky policemen. It was all over in a minute, and all that was left was the soap box and the struggling woman. . . .

From *The Nation*, September 9, 1931.

THE SCOTTSBORO BOYS

U*ntil 1931 nobody outside the little Alabama town had ever heard of Scottsboro. Then one spring day nine Negro boys were put on trial for their lives, charged with raping two white girls. The trial ended quickly. Eight were found guilty and sentenced to death in the electric chair. Outside the courthouse a band played; the crowd cheered —and what was to become a world-wide challenge to America's treatment of the Negro began.*

The NAACP supported defense of the Scottsboro boys, with churchmen, liberals, radicals joining in. All over America and in capitals around the world meetings were held to protest justice, Southern-style. Over the years there were appeals, high court reversals, new sentences, still more appeals. None of the Scottsboro boys was executed, and all were eventually freed.

It was early in the Great Depression when it all began. The boys had been bumming their way around the country in search of work. How the trouble started is told in these words of Haywood Patterson, one of the Scottsboro boys.

Scottsboro boy . . .

1931

THE FREIGHT TRAIN leaving out of Chattanooga, going around the mountain curves and hills of Tennessee into Alabama, it went so slow anyone could get off and back on.

That gave the white boys the idea they could jump off the train and pick up rocks, carry them back on, and chunk them at us Negro boys.

The trouble began when three or four white boys crossed over the oil tanker that four of us colored fellows from Chattanooga were in. One of the white boys, he stepped on my hand and liked to have knocked me off the train. I didn't say anything then, but the same guy, he brushed by me again and liked to have pushed me off the car. I caught hold of the side of the tanker to keep from falling off.

I made a complaint about it and the white boy talked back —mean, serious, white folks Southern talk.

That is how the Scottsboro case began . . . with a white foot on my black hand.

"The next time you want by," I said, "just tell me you want by and I let you by."

"Nigger, I don't ask you when I want by. What you doing on this train anyway?"

"Look, I just tell you the next time you want by you just tell me you want by and I let you by."

"Nigger bastard, this a white man's train. You better get off. All you black bastards better get off!"

I felt we had as much business stealing a ride on this train as those white boys hoboing from one place to another looking for work like us. But it happens in the South most poor whites feel they are better than Negroes and a black man has few rights. It was wrong talk from the white fellow and I felt I should sense it into him and his friends we were human beings with rights too. I didn't want that my companions, Roy and Andy Wright, Eugene Williams and myself, should get off that train for anybody unless it was a fireman or engineer or railroad dick who told us to get off.

"You white sonsofbitches, we got as much right here as you!"

"Why, you goddamn nigger, I think we better just put you off!"

"Okay, you just try. You just try to put us off!"

Three or four white boys, they were facing us four black boys now, and all cussing each other on both sides. But no fighting yet.

The white boys went on up the train further.

We had just come out of a tunnel underneath Lookout Mountain when the argument started. The train, the name of it was the Alabama Great Southern, it was going uphill now, slow. A couple of the white boys, they hopped off, picked up rocks, threw them at us. The stones landed around us and some hit us. Then the white fellows, they hopped back on the train two or three cars below us. We were going toward Stevenson, Alabama, when the rocks came at us. We got very mad.

When the train stopped at Stevenson, I think maybe to get water or fuel, we got out of the car and walked along the tracks. We met up with some other young Negroes from another car. We told them what happened. They agreed to come in with us when the train started again.

Soon as the train started the four of us Chattanooga boys that was in the oil tanker got back in there—and the white boys started throwing more rocks. The other colored guys, they came over the top of the train and met us four guys. We decided we would go and settle with these white boys. We went toward their car to fight it out. There must have been ten or twelve or thirteen of us colored when we came on a gang of six or seven white boys.

I don't argue with people. I show them. And I started to show those white boys. The other colored guys, they pitched in on these rock throwers too. Pretty quick the white boys began to lose in the fist fighting. We outmanned them in hand-to-hand scuffling. Some of them jumped off and some we put off. The train, picking up a little speed, that helped us do the job. A few wanted to put up a fight but they didn't have a chance. We had color anger on our side.

The train was picking up speed and I could see a few Negro boys trying to put off one white guy. I went down by them and told them not to throw this boy off because the train was going too fast. This fellow, his name was Orville Gilley. Me and one of the Wright boys pulled him back up.

After the Gilley boy was back on the train the fight was over. The four of us, Andy and Roy Wright, Eugene Williams and myself, we went back to the tanker and sat the same way we were riding when the train left Chattanooga.

The white fellows got plenty sore at the whupping we gave them. They ran back to Stevenson to complain that they were jumped on and thrown off—and to have us pulled off the train.

The Stevenson depot man, he called up ahead to Paint Rock and told the folks in that little through-road place to turn out in a posse and snatch us off the train.

It was two or three o'clock in the afternoon, Wednesday, March 25, 1931, when we were taken off at Paint Rock. . . .

A mob of white farmers was waiting when the train rolled in. They closed in on the boxcars. Their pistols and shotguns pointed at us. They took everything black off the train. They even threw off some lumps of coal, could be because of its color. Us nine black ones they took off from different cars. Some of these Negroes I had not seen before the fight and a couple I was looking at now for the first time. They were rounding up the whites too, about a half dozen of them. I noticed among them two girls dressed in men's overalls and looking about like the white fellows.

I asked a guy who had hold of me, "What's it all about?"

"Assault and attempt to murder."

I didn't know then there was going to be a different kind of charge after we got to the Jackson County seat, Scottsboro.

They marched us up a short road. We stopped in front of a little general store and post office. They took our names.

They roped us up, all us Negroes together. The rope stretched from one to another of us. The white folks, they looked mighty serious. Everybody had guns. The guy who ran the store spoke up for us:

"Don't let those boys go to jail. Don't anybody harm them."

But that passed quick, because we were being put into trucks. I kind of remember this man's face, him moving around there in the storm of mad white folks, talking for us. There are some good white people down South but you don't find them very fast, them that will get up in arms for a Negro. If they come up for a Negro accused of something, the white people go against him and his business goes bad.

After we were shoved into the truck I saw for the first time all us to become known as "The Scottsboro Boys." There were nine of us. Some had not even been in the fight on the train. A few in the fight got away so the posse never picked them up.

There were the four from Chattanooga, Roy Wright, about fourteen; his brother, Andy Wright, nineteen; Eugene Williams, who was only thirteen; and myself. I was eighteen. I knew the Wright boys very well. I had spent many nights at their home and Mrs. Wright treated me as if I were her own son. The other five boys, they were Olen Montgomery, he was half blind; Willie Roberson, he was so sick with the venereal he could barely move around; a fellow from Atlanta named Clarence Norris, nineteen years old; Charlie Weems, the oldest one among us, he was twenty; and a fourteen-year-old boy from Georgia, Ozie Powell. I was one of the tallest, but Norris was taller than me.

All nine of us were riding the freight for the same reason, to go somewhere and find work. It was 1931. Depression was all over the country. Our families were hard pushed. The only ones here I knew were the other three from Chattanooga. Our fathers couldn't hardly support us, and we wanted to help out, or at least put food in our own bellies by ourselves. We were freight-hiking to Memphis when the fight happened.

Looking over this crowd, I figured that the white boys got sore at the whupping we gave them, and were out to make us see it the bad way.

We got to Scottsboro in a half hour. Right away we were huddled into a cage, all of us together. It was a little two-story jimcrow jail. There were flat bars, checkerboard style, around the windows, and a little hallway outside our cell.

We got panicky and some of the kids cried. The deputies were rough. They kept coming in and out of our cells. They kept asking questions, kept pushing us and shoving, trying to make us talk. Kept cussing, saying we tried to kill off the white boys on the train. Stomped and raved at us and flashed their guns and badges.

We could look out the window and see a mob of folks gathering. They were excited and noisy. We were hot and sweaty, all of us, and pretty scared. I laughed at a couple of the guys who were crying. I didn't feel like crying. I couldn't figure what exactly, but didn't have no weak feeling.

After a while a guy walked into our cell, with him a couple of young women.

"Do you know these girls?"

They were the two girls dressed like men rounded up at Paint Rock along with the rest of us brought off the train. We had seen them being hauled in. They looked like the others, like the white hobo fellows, to me. I paid them no mind. I didn't know them. None of us from Chattanooga, the Wrights, Williams, and myself, ever saw them before Paint Rock. Far as I knew none of the nine of us pulled off different gondolas and tankers ever saw them.

"No," everybody said.

"No," I said.

"No? You damn-liar niggers! You raped these girls!"

Round about dusk hundreds of people gathered about the jailhouse. "Let these niggers out," they yelled. We could hear it coming in the window. "If you don't, we're coming in after them." White folks were running around like mad ants, white ants, sore that somebody had stepped on their hill. We heard them yelling like crazy how they were coming in after us and what ought to be done with us. "Give 'em to us," they kept screaming, till some of the guys, they cried like they were seven or eight years old. Olen Montgomery, he was seventeen and came from Monroe, Georgia, he could make the ugliest face when he cried. I stepped back and laughed at him.

As evening came on the crowd got to be about five hundred, most of them with guns. Mothers had kids in their arms. Autos, bicycles, and wagons were parked around the place. People in and about them.

Two or three deputies, they came into our cell and said, "All right, let's go." They wanted to take us out to the crowd. They handcuffed us each separately. Locked both our hands together. Wanted to rush us outside into the hands of the mob. We fellows hung close, didn't want for them to put those irons on. You could see the look in those deputies' faces, already taking some funny kind of credit for turning us over.

High Sheriff Warren—he was on our side—rushed in at those deputies and said, "Where you taking these boys?"

"Taking them to another place, maybe Gadsden or some other jail."

"You can't take those boys out there! You'll be overpowered and they'll take the boys away from you."

The deputies asked for their handcuffs back and beat it out.

That was when the high sheriff slipped out the back way himself and put in a call to Montgomery for the National Guards.

He came back to our cell a few minutes later and said, "I don't believe that story the girls told."

His wife didn't believe it either. She got busy right then and went to the girls' cell not far from ours. We all kept quiet and listened while Mrs. Warren accused them of putting down a lie on us. "You know you lied," she said, so that we heard it and so did the white boys in their cell room.

The girls stuck to their story; but us black boys saw we had some friends.

It had been a fair day, a small wind blowing while we rode on the freight. Now, toward evening, it was cool, and the crowd down there was stomping around to keep warm and wanting to make it real hot. When it was coming dark flashlights went on, and headlights from a few Fords lit up the jail. The noise was mainly from the white folks still calling for a lynching party. Every now and then one of them would yell, for us to hear, "Where's the rope, Bill?" or "Got enough rope, Hank?" They were trying to find something to help them to break into jail, begging all the while to turn us fellows over to them.

Round four o'clock in the morning we heard heavy shooting coming into the town. It was the National Guards. They were firing to let the crowd know they were coming, they meant business, and we weren't to be burned or hung. The mob got scared and fussed off and away while the state soldiers' trucks came through.

I was young, didn't know what it was all about. I believed the National Guard was some part of the lynching bee. When they came into my cell I figured like the others—that we were as good as long gone now.

First guard to walk in, he was full of fun. He asked some of the boys, "Where you want your body to go to?"

Willie Roberson, he had earlier told one of the deputies he was from Ohio, but now he took this guard serious. He said, "Send my body to my aunt at 992 Michigan Avenue, Atlanta." His aunt owned the place at that address. Others told false names, like people do at first when they're arrested.

Charlie Weems, he had a lot of guts. He understood it was a gag. He said, "Just bury me like you do a cat. Dig a hole and throw me in it."

He understood the guard was funning, but the others didn't. I didn't very well understand it myself.

After the National Guards told us they were for us, I believed them. I told them rightaway where I came from, "just over the state line, Chattanooga, Tennessee."

I don't tell people stories, I tell the truth.

I told the truth about my name and where I came from. I knew that was all right with my people, they would wade through blood for me.

And which they did.

Early the next morning we had breakfast. Then the National Guards led us out of the jail. We were going to Gadsden, Alabama, where it was supposed to be safer. Soon as we filed out of the jailhouse another mob was there screaming the same stuff at us and talking mean to the National Guards. "We're going to kill you niggers!"

"You ain't going to do a goddamned thing," I yelled back at them. That made them wild.

They sat us down among other colored prisoners at the Gadsden jail. It was the same kind of a little old jimcrow lockup as the one at Scottsboro. White guys, they were in cells a little way down the hall. We talked back and forth with them.

We waited to see what the Jackson County law was going to do with us. The Scottsboro paper had something to say about us. In big headlines, editorials and everything, they said they had us nine fiends in jail for raping two of their girls. The editor had come rummaging around the jail himself.

Then we heard that on March 31 we were indicted at Scottsboro. A trial was set for April 6, only a week away. Down around that way they'll hoe potatoes kind of slow sometimes but comes to trying Negroes on a rape charge they work fast. We had no lawyers. Saw no lawyers. We had no contact with the outside. Our folks, as far as we knew, didn't know the jam we were in. I remember the bunch of us packed in the cell room, some crying, some mad. That was a thinking time, and I thought of my mother, Jannie Patterson, and my father, Claude Patterson. I thought of my sisters and brothers and wondered if they had read about us by now.

What little we heard was going on about us we got from

the white inmates. Some were pretty good guys. They saw the papers, read them to us, and the guards talked with them. These fellows, they told us the story had got around all over Alabama and maybe outside the state. They told us, "If you ever see a good chance, you better run. They said they're going to give every one of you the death seat."

I couldn't believe that. I am an unbelieving sort.

From *Scottsboro Boy,* by Haywood Patterson
and Earl Conrad, Doubleday, 1950.

M*ore than half of America's Negroes were jobless by 1932. Misery and suffering seeped into almost every household. In the big cities there were three or four times as many Negroes on relief as whites. In Atlanta two out of three Negro workers needed public funds to keep from starving; in Norfolk it was four out of five.*

Going to the private and public agencies for relief, Negroes met Jim Crow. Some churches and charities had a "for whites only" policy in their soup kitchens. Where work relief was offered, Negroes were often left out or were paid lower wages.

If a man was lucky enough to hang on to his job during the depression, pay was usually pushed lower and lower. In some places racist groups, seeing blacks work while whites were idle, shoved in and tore away what jobs Negroes still had. In Mississippi, strong-arm methods moved to murder in 1932, when eight Negro railroad firemen were shot down because whites wanted their jobs.

Murder in Mississippi was not news. And the killing of Negroes by whites, if it did reach the courts, never resulted in convictions. It was the old custom of this "closed society," built upon the rich soil of the delta back in slavery days. Life had begun to open out a little, after military defeat in the Civil War, when there had been a brief period of Reconstruction. Then the state had known a democracy in which Negroes and poor whites were full citizens for the first time, voting, holding office, building schools, sending two Negroes to the United States Senate.

With the bloody overthrow of Reconstruction, the closed society was restored. Again the race issue was used to lock Negroes out of political and civic life—no voting, no office-holding, no jury duty, miserable schools and housing, segregation everywhere. And violence—violence threatening every hour of the day and night any Negro who dared try to pry open the tiniest crack in the closed society. The records show 533 Negroes lynched in Mississippi from 1882 to 1946. (How many quiet, casual killings have gone unrecorded?)

The murders in 1932 were done in the open, and evoked an editorial from the state's leading white newspaper. Negroes had their own comment to make, in the pages of Opportunity, *foreshadowing the militant movement that would shake Mississippi almost 30 years later.*

They wanted their jobs...

1932

RECENTLY SEVERAL white men were arrested and indicted in Mississippi for complicity in the murder of Negro firemen who were at work on the railroad systems of that state. These arrests were brought about by the insistence of railway authorities only after eight Negroes had been shot down in cold blood. Of their crime the Jackson-Mississippi *News*—an influential white daily—said:

"Their only offense was that they were holding jobs that white men evidently wanted. They were peaceful, hard-working, law-abiding Negroes entitled to the full protection of the law in their God-given right to earn their living in the sweat of their faces.

"These Negroes were our wards. They exercised but few of the rights of citizenship. They did not vote, they took no active part in civic affairs, they did not lobby in legislative halls, and they did not make themselves vocal about the prevalent depression. On the contrary they went humbly and faithfully to their daily tasks offering no protest when their wages were slashed or working hours reduced. And yet, because white men coveted their jobs, they had to die."

It may not occur to the editor of the Mississippi *News* that the reason why these unfortunate men could be shot down with impunity is precisely because "They did not vote, they took no active part in civic affairs, they did not lobby in legislative halls, they did not make themselves vocal about the prevalent depression." . . . Disfranchised—the Negro is powerless to defend himself against oppression. The logic of those who murdered black workingmen because they wanted their jobs is essentially the same process of reasoning which has deprived the Negro of the right to vote, equitable division of school funds, access to the public parks, playgrounds and libraries for the maintenance of which he is taxed the same as other citizens.

A few weeks ago the Mayor of New Orleans secured the passage of an ordinance limiting employment on the waterfront to registered voters which, if a permanent injunction had not been secured, would have thrown thousands of Negroes out of work, who have been virtually disfranchised by discriminatory administration of the election laws.

Throughout the South Negroes are being forced off jobs to make places for unemployed white men—by intimidation, coercion and murder. For the most part the public authorities are indifferent, the press silent, the pulpit dumb. It is a dangerous situation fraught with untold possibilities of disaster.

"To tolerate such a condition of affairs"—continues the *News*—"means that our own children will grow up without respect for law and order. Worse still it means we are heading for anarchy."

We would not withhold our commendation of the *News* for this candid statement. At the same time we wonder whether its concern for the future generations includes the black children of that sovereign state. If contempt for the rights of citizens provokes disrespect for law and order and invites anarchy, then the future of Mississippi, judged by its past, is dark indeed.

From *Opportunity*, October, 1932.

B*ad as the depression years* *were for Negroes in the Northern cities, in the South it was* *even worse. Life in the 1930s on the farms of the South—* *perhaps the most stagnant backwater of the economy—was* *depicted in* The Shadow of the Plantation. *It was the work of* *Charles S. Johnson, one of the most productive of the Negro* *social scientists.*

The scientific study of Negro life and history began well *before the Civil War. Such Negroes as William C. Nell, James* *McCune Smith, William Wells Brown, Martin Delany, and* *George Washington Williams were the forerunners of scholars* *who came on the scene later. Many of these later contributors* *to research were members of the Negro American Academy, founded by Alexander Crummell. Foremost among them was W. E. B. DuBois, with a great many distinguished and often pioneering studies to his credit in both history and sociology. He was followed by Carter G. Woodson, the dean of Negro historians.*

Woodson wrote many histories himself, and launched the Association for the Study of Negro Life and History and its chief publication, the Journal of Negro History. *Both sought to promote race pride by researching and teaching the facts of Negro history.*

Born in Virginia in 1893, Charles Johnson was educated at Virginia Union University and the University of Chicago. While research director for the National Urban League, he founded and edited its publication, Opportunity: Journal of Negro Life. *He had already helped prepare a study of the Negro in Chicago, and in 1928, moving to Nashville to become head of the social science department at Fisk University, he entered one of his most fruitful periods.*

Among the studies he prepared was a report on plantation life. It appeared in 1934, in the midst of the depression. In this passage from the book the Negro farmers often speak for themselves.

Ain't make nothing,
don't speck nothing...
1934

TENANT FARMERS

"I AIN'T GOT NO children and me and my husband works a one-horse farm and we got 'bout thirty acres. Last year we made 6 bales of cotton and rented the thirty acres for $60; fifteen acres we used for cotton, the rest for corn. We kept the corn and didn't sell none hardly. At ten cents a pound the six bales would bring $300. We had $10 advanced for four months. We turned it all over, and they took out the $40 advances, $30 for fertilizer, and $60 rent. We got through and then they say we come out $72.43 in the hole. . . ."

In more prosperous times when there is a reasonable assurance of returns, the landowners made advances both to tenants and to sharecroppers. It is a most frequent complaint of the tenants now that they cannot get advances. One said: "I ask Mr. —— to 'vance me jest nuff for a pair of overalls. He tell me he needs overalls hisself." In other cases advances to tenants have merely been reduced.

"Last year I drawed $10 to the plow (meaning $10 a

month for from four to six months for each 20 acres cultivated) but I ain't getting but $7 this year. I rents the whole
place (400 acres) and then subrents it, and pays four bales
of cotton for rent. But I don't never make nothing offen it.
Didn't clear nothing last year. I paid out $200 last year. In-
terest steps on me time I pay me rent (for money borrowed
from the bank) and interest cost 15 cents on the dollar. I
haven't made nothing since 1927. I clears $210 then and ain't
cleared nothing since. I got 21 cents for cotton that year."

Another explained: "They don't give nothing now. Use to
'low us $10 provisions a month, but dey done cut us way
down. The white folks say some of these banks done fell in;
dere ain't no money to be got. That's all. Said this is the suppression time."

Another type of tenant pays a good rental in cash and re-
ceives advances.

"We farms 60 acres and pays $150 for rent. That's $75
to the plow. They 'vances us $15 a month for five months.
I come out jest $175 in the hole.

"We run a two-horse farm. We was due to pay $150 rent
last year, but I don't know what us is paying this year. We
cut down on the land we was using. We made 22 bales of
cotton last year, and it was selling at 8, 9, and 10 cents when
we turned it in to the man. We didn't git nothing back. You
see, the man had been carrying us for two years. I took 'spon-
sibility for the whole patch and let some of it out to three other
parties, and stood for them. Besides the cotton the men took
13 loads of corn, but I saved about 200 bushels for myself to
live on, and I sold some peanuts and corn."

The normal earning of a man and wife, if both work as

tenants on a one-horse cotton farm, would probably average $260 a year in cash value. However, they pay about half of their cotton in rent, use the corn for their stock, and eat the potatoes, peas, and sorghum which they grow along with the cotton. As a result very little cash is handled. They manage to live on the advances, or by borrowing for food and clothing and permitting their crop to be taken in satisfaction of the debt. It becomes very largely a paper loss or gain. In the case of loss the tenant may move away, leaving his debt. In the latter case he may be conscious of having earned more than he got, or of paying for some other Negro tenant's default.

"We got right 'round sixty acres and one-half of it is cotton. We working on halves. We got a two-horse farm. My daughter got one and I got one. I farmed with Mr. P—— last year. We had thirty acres over there and made 5 bales of cotton and paid $100 for rent. We gits $2 a month in cash and $10 in rations. We came out $200 in the hole last year. I don't have to pay off 'cause I let that went when I come here (he had to give up farm tools, etc.). I been farming all my life 'cept two years when we went to Virginia . . . I worked in the coke field out there. That was the year the war was."

One daughter lived at home. Four boys were away living in cities in Alabama. One grown daughter lived in the county and worked with them. One grown son was dead—"got knocked in the head"; seven little children had died between the ages of two and four.

SHARECROPPERS

There is another type of farmer, the share-cropper, who, without tools or any form of capital, farms on the condition that he give the landlord one-half of the crop. . . . The arrangement varies with the landlord and the condition of the tenant. When the tenant is furnished tools and work animals in addition to the land, he may get only a third of the cotton raised. Most commonly, however, it is halves, and he may find it necessary to rent a mule for his plowing.

The share-croppers frequently are subtenants for small white and Negro tenant farmers, or for their relatives. It is at least a means of beginning, and a good share-cropper can, with good fortune, place himself in position to undertake the responsibilities of full tenant later.

"I works a one-horse farm on halves. I get 'bout $12 a month in rations. Last year I worked for the Tallahassee Mill Company, and made $9.75 a week. My wife was working by the day for 50 cents a day. We been married 'bout four years now. I moved here from Tallahassee 'cause I was lacking for sense. The white folks liked me down there and everything, and I moved. I called myself liking ter farm best."

FARM LABORERS

Farm laborers worked on other people's farms for a stipulated wage. [They] had small patches of their own which they were permitted to cultivate rent free. The wage usually paid these laborers was 50-65 cents a day, the women receiving more often 40 cents. The following statement of a farm laborer indicates the conditions under which this class works.

"We jest work by the day and pay $1.50 a month for this house. It's jest a piece of house. I gits 50 cents a day and my husband and the boy gits 65 cents each. We have to feed ourselves and pay rent out of that. My husband is pretty scheming, but sometimes he can't git nothing to do. I don't know how much time we lose, but he works most of the time. Course the boy stops and goes to school in the winter sometimes, but if he can git work to do, he works too." . . .

Among these families there were also laborers who were working on railroads, logging, and on county roads. . . . The wife of one of these laborers related the following history:

"My husband and me married eight years. He works at the Hardaway log mill and makes $7 a week. He been working there four years now. . . . We don't have to pay no rent. The man he works for pays for hit. I don't do nothing but stay home. . . . My husband was in debt when we left Millstead but he ain't much in debt now. He don't owe but 'bout a dollar or two. He don't lack this man he's working for 'cause he don't pay him but $1.10 a day. The man's name is Mr. S—— and he is mean to work for. He got 14 or 15 working for him down there at the log mill 'sides my husband. If we git hard up and want some money, he don't help us. He don't do nothing but run you away from there. . . My husband goes ter work wid sunrise every morning and works till dark. I git up day and cooks his breakfast. He don't come back home ter dinner cause hit's so far. Hit's 'bout seven miles from here."

CASUALS

Probably the lowest class of farm laborers was made up of farm hands who did not receive a stipulated monetary wage, but were to get what was known as a "hand's share." This, seemingly, just amounts to enough to keep them living. One old woman who lives by herself in a one-room shack and works for a hand's share told the following story:

"I works for a hand's share in the crop with the folks cross dere. My husband been dead. I ain't never had but one child and dat's de son what's down there. . . . I been up north in Birmingham with my sister . . . but I come back here, 'cause dese chillun kept worrying me to come on here to live wid them. It's mighty tight on me to have to go working in dese fields half starved, and I ain't had a bit of money to buy a piece of cloth as big as my hand since I been back. I washed fer white people in Birmingham, and dey was good to me. I am jest gitting long by the hardest. I works for dese people for a hand's share in the crop. Dey gives me a load of corn and a load of potatoes. I gits some of all the other stuff what's made, and when selling cotton dey give you a little money out of the seed, I don't see no money on time. Dey gives me a little something to eat 'cause I works wid dem and dey gives me a little groceries. I never was in this fix before in my life. I had good money when I come from Birmingham. I had two fives and five single dollahs. I sho' gonna git what I works for dis year." . . .

THE DREARY CYCLE OF LIFE

The weight of generations of habit holds the Negro tenant to his rut. Change is difficult, even in the face of the increasing struggle for survival under the old modes. One intelligent old farmer had sensed an important element of the natural conservatism of these tenants. He said:

"Farming is like gambling. If I get out I ought to get back and work a smaller farm next year. But you take an old farmer and if he ever gets out the hole with a good-size farm, instead of cutting down he'll get him another mule and take on some more. That's what keeps us down."

Such philosophy is for the man who retains some hope for improvement. The most dismal aspect of this situation is the air of resignation everywhere apparent.

"If it wasn't the boll weevil it was the drought; if it wasn't the drought it was the rains.

"One thing, we ain't got proper tools we ought to have. If you git any good land you have to buy things to make it good, and that takes lots of money, and if we had money to buy these things we wouldn't be so hard up.

"What kills us here is that we jest can't make it cause they pay us nothing for what we give them, and they charge us double price when they sell it back to us."

Year after year of this experience for many of them and the hopelessness crystallizes itself at times into despair. "Ain't make nothing, don't speck nothing no more till I die. Eleven bales of cotton and man take it all. We jest work for de other man. He git everything." Mysticism and religion come to the rescue of some who add to hopelessness a fear of the future.
"I axed Jesus to let me plant a little more. Every time I plant anything I say, 'Jesus, I ain't planting this for myself; I'm planting this for you to increase.' " . . .

Henry Robinson had been living in the same place for nineteen years, paying $105 a year rent for his land. He raises three bales of cotton a year, turns it all over, and continues to go deeper in debt. He said:

"I know we been beat out of money direct and indirect. You see, they got a chance to do it all right, 'cause they can overcharge us and I know it's being done. I made three bales again last year. He said I owed $400 the beginning of the year. Now you can't dispute his word. When I said 'Suh?' he said 'Don't you dispute my word; the book says so.' When the book says so and so you better pay it, or they will say 'So, I'm a liar, eh?' You better take to the bushes too if you dispute him, for he will string you up for that.

"I don't want them to hurt my feelings and I just have to take what they say, 'cause I don't want to go to the mines [convict labor] and I do want to live."

Another man complained:

"I tried keeping books one year, and the man kept worrying me about it, saying his books was the ones he went by anyhow. And nothing you can do but leave. He said he didn't have no time to fool with no books. He don't ever give us no rent notes all the time. They got you 'cause you have to carry your cotton to his mill to gin and you better not carry your cotton nowhere else. I don't care how good your cotton is, a colored man's cotton is always second- or third-grade cotton if a colored man sells it. The only way you can get first prices for it is to get some white man to sell it for you in his name. A white man sold mine once, and got market price for it.

"We haven't paid out to Mr. —— in twelve years. Been in debt that long. See, when a fella's got a gun in your face you gotter take low or die."

To the Negro tenant the white landlord is the system; to the white landlord the capital of the banks is the system. The landlord needs credit by which to advance credit to the tenants. The security of the landlord is in the mortgages on his land; the security of the tenant is the mortgage on the crops which he will raise. Because cotton lends itself best to this arrangement, cotton is overproduced and debts descend to obscure still another year of labor, and the vicious circle continues. In the desperate struggle both may lose, but the advantage is always with the white landlord. He dictates the terms and keeps the books. The demands of the system determine the social and economic relations, the weight of which falls heaviest upon those lowest down. There was a song which old women hummed as they hacked the earth with their hoes. The words were almost always indistinct but the mood of the tune, dreary and listless, fitted as naturally to the movement of their bodies as it did to the slick and swish of the earth under the blows of their hoes. One verse only was remembered by one of them, and it ran so:

> *Trouble comes, trouble goes.*
> *I done had my share of woes.*
> *Times get better by 'n' by,*
> *But then my time will come to die.*

From *The Shadow of the Plantation,* by Charles S. Johnson,
University of Chicago Press, 1934.

The millions of rural Negroes who have left the South in this century have shunned farm labor in the North. They came away to escape the life they had known, not to renew its miseries somewhere else. Hardly one per cent of all the nation's Negro farmers live outside the region of the old South. Few have seen any future for themselves in farming.

Some Negroes in the North have worked on farms as hired hands. In the 1930s, migrants running from the depression tried to make a living in the vast agricultural valleys of California. Others settled on farms in Michigan or Ohio, and some moved with the crops through the Middle Atlantic farming sections.

The hired farm laborer has always been at the bottom of the economic ladder. He rated the smallest pay and got the least respect. He was often out of work between seasons; his education was a scrap if anything; and most of the basic protections other workers now take for granted—minimum wages and hours, unemployment insurance, disability compensation— were denied him. Black or white, the farm worker has been almost a social outcast, an untouchable. And because the job's status is so low, Negroes have been heavily used.

In 1934, Negro farm laborers in New Jersey, suffering under feudal conditions, made a choice that created a national sensation. They did not give in to an intolerable life, nor did they migrate: they struck to make life better. Opportunity *sent Lester B. Granger to find out what was happening and why.*

Granger, whose father was a doctor and whose mother was a school teacher, enjoyed unsegregated schooling in New Jersey but met discrimination at Dartmouth College. He served in World War I, took graduate training in social work, and then joined the staff of the Urban League, becoming its director in 1941.

In his report Granger shows how long-suppressed anger and bitterness were channelled into the kind of social protest that was beginning to sweep the depression-ridden country.

So why not strike? . . .
1934

"DID WE WIN the strike? Brother, I don't know, and that's a fact," said Jim Mills. "I know we didn't lose it. We ain't got nothin' now, maybe, but we didn't have nothin' befo'—so how could we lose?"

And that in general is the attitude of the rest of the Negro farm and cannery workers of Bridgeton, N.J., strikers and non-strikers, as they take stock of their situation during the aftermath of . . . the Bridgeton strike, a dramatic walkout and more dramatic picketing by 300 white and Negro employees of the 5000-acre Seabrook Farm. The strike broke upon the metropolitan area with astounding unexpectedness; it tied up New Jersey's largest farming section for a thrilling two weeks, it cost the farm owners a crop loss of $100,000, it set Negro and white women and men battling shoulder to shoulder against police and sheriff's deputies armed with shot guns, clubs and tear gas bombs.

Such events seemed almost unbelievable to those who knew Bridgeton as the quiet and picturesque county seat of Cumberland County. Tourists from Wilmington to Atlantic City remembered the town as a prosperous community of 20,000, surrounded by rich farms and presenting wide, shaded streets and attractive homes to the passing motorists. . . .

Many Negroes know Bridgeton, also, for they have read of historical Gouldtown with its thrifty group of colored small farmers, descendants of pre-Revolutionary settlers. They have visited the town for week-ends to picnic in the attractive groves and to bathe in the countless swimming holes which the adjacent river and ponds afford. They have heard that Bridgeton colored folk are "backward"—that they live in terrible houses, that they are content to work for three and four dollars a week, that no colored physician has been able to make a living from the 2,000 Negroes resident in town and country nearby.

Bridgeton lives twenty years behind the times. Even the Ku Klux Klan is still active hereabout. The knights of the hooded sheet own meeting groves and gather for "konklaves" and burn crosses for the mystification of a bucolic audience. The entire county is controlled industrially, politically and socially by a small group of cannery, glass factory and farm owners—of which last class Charles F. Seabrook is one.

Bridgeton is pleasant to see, with its old-fashioned homes of colonial architecture and its wide shaded streets, but the social soul of the town is not so pretty. That soul may be found by turning off the main streets into the back alleys where live the workers in canneries, in homes and on farms. At first sight these neighborhoods give a shock. Half-clothed, half-starved, completely dirty children, poor white and Negro, run about in hopelessly squalid surroundings. Frowsy heads looks out from half-open doors, through which may be seen barely ventilated

rooms crowded with broken furniture and with broken humanity. . . . An acrid odor lingers everywhere—the odor which
spells no running water, no toilets, no fit habitation for
humans.

"Sure!" says the family head. "The water's cut off—been cut
off ever since we been here. The roof leaks in all the rooms but
this'n. Rent? We pays ten a month.

"I makes 'bout seven-fifty a week in pickin' time and the
boy, he gin'ally make most as much, but he been sickly the
las' few weeks. The wife, she do's day's work and she make
'bout three a week, so we mostly gits along someways."

It was out of situations like this, to be found among Negro
and Italian pickers in the fields and workers in the canneries,
that the strike idea was born in all defiance of South Jersey
public attitudes, in all defiance of Klan threats, in all defiance
of the traditional belief that Negroes will not strike and that
Negroes and whites cannot organize together successfully.

The Bridgeton strike was news, dramatic news for the metropolitan dailies which found amazing the spectacle of Negroes actually organizing to strike and to defy the armed might
of Cumberland County's police forces. . . . Two hundred
and fifty strikers were on the picket line outside the farm
gates, determined that scabs should not go in to work the crops
and that trucks should not come out to take their loads to
market. The presence of town police, sheriff's deputies, and
fifty or more volunteer "vigilantes" recruited from white farmers of the section failed to awe the strikers in the least. As
trucks attempted to roll out of the grounds, men and women
climbed on top and threw the vegetable loads to the ground.

Police grappled with the raiders, and were themselves attacked by picket reinforcements. Women received and gave no quarter in the hand-to-hand scuffling. Tear gas bombs were brought into play and the police gained a temporary advantage which enabled them to arrest twenty-seven strikers, about half of them Negroes, and hustle them into Bridgeton to the county jail. This was the story which intrigued the press of three great cities, which focussed public attention upon the disgraceful conditions under which men and women work in South Jersey's farms, and which brought Federal and state mediators to the scene to arrange for strike settlement.

Behind this story was the real story of how Jerry Brown, Negro farmhand, together with Dan Hart, Casey Jones, Robert Swigley and Joseph Sicosi, got together to organize white and Negro workers who were toiling in the fields ten hours a day to make a wage of $1.75 at night fall. . . .

[In] the first strike on April 10th . . . Jerry Brown, as president of the Agricultural and Cannery Workers' Industrial Union, was fired by Seabrook for his organizing activities. Seabrook was forced to deal with Jerry after all, for the workers walked out in a body and named Brown as leader of their committee.

"Jerry," said Seabrook, "you know we've always been for the colored people. You know we've always hired them on our farms right along with the white folks."

"Yes," says Jerry, "hired 'em last and fired 'em first when slack season comes along."

"Break up the union," urged Seabrook, "and I'll take care of you. I'll fire all the Dagoes and just keep colored on. I'd rather have colored anyhow."

And so on, through all the traditional employer-to-worker

arguments. In the long run, the strikers went back to work, not for seventeen and a half cents an hour, but under a new agreement which paid twenty-five cents to women and thirty cents to men. They worked on that basis until June 25th, when notice came to the workers' union that the farm owners simply could not pay such wages and make a profit and that the rate would be cut to twenty, eighteen, and fifteen cents an hour for men, women and children.

Moreover, the workers found that another agreement was being violated. It had been the Seabrook custom, during the slack season, to lay off most of his Negro help and to keep on the white workers. This, in conference with the union, he had promised not to do, but to keep on workers without regard to race. The June lay-off, however, found 125 workers dropped, with nearly all of them Negroes. The lay-off and the wage cut roused the workers' indignation afresh, and a second strike was called. . . .

A group sat in the colored Elks Hall and, chairs tilted back against the wall, summed up the situation.

"The way I look at it is like this," said one, a towering truck driver. "I've been hanging around this town a good while—too damned long. I've never seen a colored man get anything for his work but a beating. He works his head off all day long, and all he's got is enough to eat on. If he don't work, he's no worse off, because the relief won't let him starve anyhow.

"I say, if we can't get anything for working, let's see what we can get for fighting. This ain't the only town in God's country. If we can't make it here, we'll let these pecks have the town. But we'll make 'em sweat for it first!"

From *Opportunity*, August, 1934.

The hard work and the dirty work—that has traditionally been the lot of the Negro. It remained true into the 1960s, when over 70 per cent of Negro men and women held unskilled or semiskilled jobs, chiefly in the service or farm occupations. If you took the 11 largest occupations for Negro men, only one—auto mechanic and repairman—was above the semiskilled level. And Negro women were bunched even more tightly in a few lower-level jobs, especially as domestic workers.

Negroes who came North during the twenties broke into new fields of work—glass, tobacco, paper, clothing, food. But whites did not open the unions to them. Many branches of the American Federation of Labor refused to enroll them or *shunted them into Jim Crow locals. The NAACP and the Urban League made progress in these years, but chiefly among the small black middle class. The millions of Negroes whose problems were largely getting enough to eat and a decent place to live were not reached. Only among the Pullman car porters was a solid union organized—in 1925, under the leadership of A. Philip Randolph.*

It was not until the frantic first years of the New Deal that the Negro labor force began to move into the unions. Many new measures were devised by the Roosevelt regime to combat the depression. The work week was shortened; children under 16 were forbidden to work; a minimum wage was set; a federal relief plan created jobs by the millions. A vast public works program built new hospitals, schools, community centers, and playgrounds all over the land. Negroes got jobs in several of the work programs, but not in proportion to their actual need. In the South, wages paid Negroes were lower than those paid whites.

By now the basic industries of the country had swelled to gigantic size. Mass production brought thousands of workers into auto and steel plants, into meatpacking, rubber, electrical goods. The intricate machines could be run by unskilled or semiskilled hands. Pay was low, speedup was intense, jobs were insecure. Millions were ripe for organization, but the old unions, formed by crafts, could not take on the mass production industries. It was then that a new law passed by the Roosevelt Congress gave labor "the right to organize and bargain collectively through representatives of their own choosing."

It was a rebirth for labor. Feeling they had the President's blessing, organizers fanned out over the country, recruiting thousands of new members into the unions. Both the American Federation of Labor and the new Congress of Industrial Organizations grew with tremendous speed. Within a few years the CIO embraced 32 national unions with four million members.

It took great strikes to win recognition of the unions. Picket lines seemed to stretch from one coast to the other. What the new unions meant to Negro workers in Southern industry is told in two selections. In the first, Ted Poston, one of the first Negro reporters to break through Jim Crow in journalism, went to Richmond to talk to the tobacco workers. In the second, Henry O. Mayfield of Birmingham tells what it was like to organize in the mines and foundries in the 1930s.

We gonna make this a union town yet!...

1930s

RICHMOND, VA.

SHE WAS A SCRAWNY hardbitten little woman and she greeted me with that politely blank stare which Negroes often reserve for hostile whites or prying members of their own race.

I had been directed to her tenement in Richmond's ramshackle Negro section by another woman, a gray-haired old grandmother whose gnarled hands had been stemming tobacco for five decades.

"The white folks down at union headquarters is all right," she had said, "and we love 'em—especially Mr. Marks. But if you want to know about us stemmers and the rumpus we raised, you better go see Mamma Harris. She's Missus CIO in Richmond."

The blank look softened on the thin dark face when I mentioned this.

"Must've been Sister Jones," she said, still standing near

the door. "They all call me Mamma though. Even if I ain't but forty-nine and most of 'em old enough to be my grand-mammy."

I edged toward a rocking chair in the other side of the bed.

"I'm a CIO man myself," I remarked. "Newspaper Guild. Our local boys just fixed up *The Times-Dispatch* this morning."

She yelled so suddenly that I almost missed the rocker.

"Bennie!" she called toward the kitchen, "you hear that, Bennie? CIO's done organized *The Dispatch*. Moved right in this morning. What I tell you? We gonna make this a union town yet!"

A hulking overalled Negro appeared in the kitchen door-way. His booming bass voice heightened his startling resemblance to Paul Robeson.

"Dispatch?" he thundered. "God Amighty, we do come on."

Mrs. Harris nodded in my direction.

"He's a CIO man from up New York. Wants to know about our rumpus out at Export. He's a Guilder too, just like the white 'uns."

Benny limped toward the other chair.

"They give us hell," he said, "but we give it right back to 'em. And it was we'uns who come out on top. The cops was salty. Wouldn't even let us set down and rest. But I told the women, I told 'em 'Sit down' and they did. Right in front of the cops too. Didn't I, Louise?"

Mrs. Harris nodded energetically from her perch on the bed.

"You dead did. And they didn't do nothing neither. They 'fraid of the women. You can outtalk the men. But us women don't take no tea for the fever."

Bennie boomed agreement. "There was five hundred of the women on the picket line and only twenty of us mens. But we sure give 'em hell. I talked right up to them cops, didn't I, Louise? Didn't I?"

Finally Mrs. Harris got around to the beginning.

"I wasn't no regular stemmer at first," she said, "but I been bringing a shift somewhere or other since I was eight. I was took out of school then and give a job minding chillun. By the time I was ten I was cooking for a family of six. And I been scuffling ever since.

"But I don't work in no factory till eight years ago. Then I went out to Export. Well, it took me just one day to find out that preachers don't know nothing about hell. They ain't worked in no tobacco factory."

Bennie was smiling to himself and gazing at the ceiling.

"Them cops beat up them strikers something awful out at Vaughn's," he said. "They even kicked the women around. But they didn't do it to us, huh, Louise? We stood up to 'em."

Mrs. Harris waved aside the interruption.

"Then there was this scab," she went on, "only he ain't no scab then, cause we don't have no union. We ain't even heerd of no union nowhere but I knew something was bound to happen. Even a dog couldn't keep on like we was. You know what I make then? Two dollars and eighty cents a week. Five dollars was a too bad week."

"I put in eighty-two and a half hours one week," Bennie said, "and they only give me $18.25. I think about this one day when one of them cops . . ."

Mrs. Harris shushed him.

"Now this scab—only he ain't no scab then—he rides me

from the minute I get to Export. He's in solid with the man and he always brag he's the ringtail monkey in this circus. He's a stemmer like the rest of us but he stools for the white folks.

"There's two hundred of us on our floor alone and they only give us four and a half and five cents a pound. We don't get paid for the tobacco leaf, you know. You only get paid for the stems. And some of them stems is so puny they look like horse hair."

Bennie was chuckling softly to himself but a glance from Mrs. Harris held the cops at bay for the moment.

"And as if everything else wasn't bad enough, there was this scab. We's cramped up on them benches from kin to can't, and he's always snooping around to see nobody don't pull the stem out the center instead of pulling the leaf down both sides separate. This dust just eats your lungs right out you. You start dying the day you go in."

She coughed automatically and continued.

"Well, I keep this up for six long years. And this scab is riding me ever' single day. He's always riding everybody and snitching on them what don't take it. He jump me one day about singing. Course, a stemmer's bench ain't no place for singing and I ain't got no voice nohow. But I like a song and I gotta do something to ease my mind or else I go crazy.

"But he jump me this morning and tell me to shut up. Well, that's my cup. Six years is six years, but this once is too often. So I'm all over him like gravy over rice. I give him a tongue-lashing what curled every nap on his head."

For a moment she had the same beaming look which Bennie displayed when he spoke of the cops.

"I sass him deaf, dumb and blind, and he takes it. But all

the time he's looking at me kinder queer. And all at once he says 'You mighty salty all of a sudden' you must be joining up with this union foolishness going on around here.'

"You coulda knocked me over with a Export stem. I ain't even heard nothing about no union. But as soon as he cuts out, I start asking around. And bless my soul if they ain't been organizing for a whole full week. And I ain't heerd a peep."

"I ain't heerd nothing neither then," Benny put, "and I been there fifteen years."

Mrs. Harris caught another breath.

"Well, I don't only go to the next meeting downtown, but I carries sixty of the girls from our floor. They remember how I sass this scab and they're all with me. We plopped right down in the first row of the gallery. And when they asked for volunteers to organize Export, I can't get to my feet quick enough."

"I come in right after," Bennie remarked.

"And it ain't no time," Mrs. Harris continued, "before we got seven hundred out of the thousand what works in Export. The man is going crazy mad and the scab is snooping overtime. But they can't fire us. The boom time is on and the warehouse is loaded to the gills."

She paused dramatically.

"And then on the first of August, 1938, we let 'em have it. We called our strike and closed up Export tight as a brass drum."

Bennie couldn't be shushed this time.

"The cops swooped down like ducks on a June bug," he said, "but we was ready for 'em. I was picket captain and there was five hundred on the line. And all five hundred was black and evil."

144

Mrs. Harris was beaming again.

"Then this scab came up with a couple hundred others and tried to break our line," she recalled, "but we wasn't giving a crip a crutch or a dog a bone. I made for that head scab personal—but the cops wouldn't let me at 'em."

"I stayed on the line for twenty-four hours running," Bennie chuckled, "and I didn't take a inch from none of them cops."

"And we wasn't by ourselves neither," Mrs. Harris went on. "The preachers, Dr. Jackson, the Southern Aid Society and all the other union people help us. GWU and them garment ladies give us a hundred dollars right off the bat. Malgamate sent fifty. The ship folks down in Norfolk come through, and your white Guild boys here give ten dollars too."

"It was them white garment ladies what sent the cops," Bennie cut in. "They come out five hundred strong and parade around the factory. They got signs saying 'GWU Supports Export Tobacco Workers.'

"Them cops jump salty as hell. 'White women,' they say, 'white women out here parading for niggers.' But they don't do nothing. Because we ain't taking no stuff from nobody."

"We was out eighteen days," Mrs. Harris said, "and the boss was losing money hand over fist. But you know how much we spend in them eighteen days? Over seven hundred dollars."

Her awed tones made it sound like seven thousand.

"But it was worth it. We win out and go back getting ten, eleven and twelve cents a pound. And better still we can wear our union buttons right out open. We might even have got them scabs fired if we wanted, but we didn't want to keep nobody out of work."

Bennie stopped smiling for the first time.

"We might be better off if we did," he said soberly. "I bet we do next time."

Mrs. Harris explained.

"They been sniping away at us ever since we win. They give the scabs all the breaks and lay off us union people first whenever they can. They give all the overtime to the scabs and even let 'em get away with stripping the stem down the center. But we ain't licked yet. We still got two hundred members left and we still got union conditions."

Her face brightened again.

"And we fixed that old scab—even if he is been there nineteen years. We moved him off our floor completely, and he ain't allowed to ride nobody.

"We got a good set of people downtown now and we're reorganizing right along. By the time our new contract comes up in June, we'll probably have the whole thousand."

"And if we strike again, and them cops jump salty"—Bennie began.

And this time Mamma Harris let him pursue the subject to his heart's content.

From *New Republic*, November 4, 1940.

BIRMINGHAM, ALA.

I worked seven years in the biggest foundry in Birmingham, the Stockham Pipe and Fitting Company. Many of us worked twelve to fourteen hours daily. One worker drove a mule hauling fresh sand into the foundry and cleaned up scrap metal. After the mule worked nine hours the worker had to take the mule to the stable and get a wheel barrow and finish the work. I remember one afternoon about 4:30 P.M. the foundry superintendent told the mule driver, "You can work all the overtime you want to but I don't want the mule working one damn minute overtime." The mule driver, Nash, said, "O.K. Mr. Lynn." Nash pushed a wheelbarrow until about 9:30 that night. . . .

The conditions in the mines were very bad. Back in the early thirties we were loading coal by the ton. The company had handpicked men and gave them the contract which we had to work for the contractors. From week to week, or day to day, you never knew how much money you were going to make. Many days we stayed in the mines nine and ten hours and made only four or five dollars, sometimes less or nothing, because when you loaded a car you had no way of knowing how many tons of coal were in the car. You had to take the word of the company and the contractor. Many of the miners lived in the company's houses and had to trade at the company's stores because they seldom had any cash to trade at other stores. Clothes for the family were out of the question. The iron ore miners had to work under the same conditions as the coal miners.

The working conditions in steel and foundry were just as bad. But there was a difference in pay from the point of knowing how much you made at the end of the week. In steel and foundry the average hourly pay for Negro workers was about fifty cents an hour and you had to work from "can see to can't see . . ." (as long as the boss wanted you to work). If you asked the boss for pay for overtime, he would say that if you didn't like your pay, there were others willing to take it, or if you were a very good worker and the boss liked you, he would give you a few hours overtime and tell you not to tell the other workers.

In 1932 the United Mine Workers of America (headed by John L. Lewis), and the Mine, Mill and Smelter Workers Union, started an organizing drive to organize coal and ore miners. . . . The bloody battle was on. We had to get a small group of workers together, sometimes meeting in the woods. The companies organized armed thugs to track us down and they would shoot to kill. The ore miners had shooting battles with the company thugs and men were shot on both sides.

The workers rallied to the union around the following demands: eight-hour day and five-day week, higher pay for tonnage or day labor, to do away with contractors, two pay-days a month (instead of one pay monthly), upgrading of Negroes as motormen, machine operators and crew leaders, union members to watch the weight of the company scale for those workers loading coal or ore by the ton and, last but not least, recognition of the union.

The company countered with a "company union" which appealed in the main to the white workers. . . . We called the company union a "popsicle union" because when they started the organizing, they told the Birmingham families they would be served popsicles and watermelon. . . . We kept on fighting. . . . Many Negro workers were fired because they were leaders in the union. After the company saw we were going to win, they wanted to make a deal with some of the Negro leadership. I worked in the largest coal mine of U.S. Steel in Birmingham. I took up grievances which cost the company thousands of dollars. The superintendent called me into the office and told me if I dropped the grievances, he would see that I made all the money I wanted. I told them I will starve with the other men until this condition is corrected. . . .

Some of the men serving on grievance committees could not read or write; but they knew what to talk about when they met with the boss, and they were "tough" and would never back down. During contract time the Negro workers took the lead in working out the contracts. The few white workers in the locals were afraid to attend meetings or serve on committees. . . .

We organized women's auxiliaries in the coal and ore mines. When we were on strike the women would organize into groups and take baskets and go into stores asking for food for needy families and when they asked a storekeeper for help he knew not to say "no." . . . The young boys would be on the picket lines while the girls went out asking for food for the families. . . .

From *Freedomways,* Winter, 1964.

Young Americans growing up
in the 1960s may have had the feeling that the Freedom
Movement was like nothing else that had ever happened before. In some ways, and very important ones, that is true. But
there has been defiance of bondage ever since the mutinies
aboard the first slave ships. People in the past—as in the days
of the abolitionists—have committed themselves to the struggle against injustice and have risked all for freedom and human rights.

The South of the 1930s knew "agitators" and "trouble

makers." The cracks opened up in the social structure by the upheaval of the depression made many feel this was a time "to plan a new design for living." Local organizations of young Negroes fed delegates into regional assemblies and in 1937 the first all-South Negro youth conference took place. A year later came a second session, this time at Chattanooga, where 500 young Negroes met to discuss what they wanted and plan a program to achieve it. One of the delegates tells what was on their minds.

We want to live . . .

1938

. . . WE WHO ARE YOUNG, and who live in the South, want first of all the right to vote. We want the opportunity to serve on juries, to participate in the primary elections of all parties, to be eligible for appointment to all Federal, state, and municipal positions, and to be acceptable as candidates for public office.

To become voters is, of course, a major task. The barriers that we must overcome include abuse of the poll tax, misuse of literacy tests, the continuance of property qualifications and the misinterpretation of state constitutions by the courts. To surmount these obstacles, we realize, we must acquaint ourselves thoroughly with the laws that govern voting in our respective states, so that we first may vote ourselves, and then assist the masses of Negro people to vote. At the same time, we must organize poll-tax paying clubs and registration centers in every neighborhood to develop the maximum immediate Negro vote possible under existing conditions, and to broaden the base of that vote at each election.

It is as important, we feel, that we win the right to vote in the party primaries as in the general elections because in most sections of the South victory in the Democratic primary is synonymous with election. This right can only be secured when the U.S. Supreme Court reverses its decision which held the primaries to be private affairs. The recent addition of liberal judges to the bench may bring a reversal if somehow a new primary case can be presented.

A second thing we want is work. Three-quarters of a million of us are now out of school and unemployed. The very existence of the NYA and the CCC is threatened all the time by budget cuts. How to get jobs? How to win economic security? That is one of our major problems.

We feel that the trade-union movement must stand at the heart of any program that we may adopt. That is why we urge further unionization of Negroes and the encouragement of their active participation in bona-fide labor unions, although at the same time we recognize and condemn the openly discriminatory policies of some unions. We want the unions to give us an adequate vocational guidance program and an opportunity for apprenticeship training. We ourselves must work for the further opening up of job opportunities for Negro youth in the Federal, state and local governments, and in private industry.

We want more opportunity for education. We realize that such a program must contain plans to assist Negro youth financially in their efforts to go to school and so we hope for the passage of the American Youth Act which would provide Federal assistance to help the states solve their educational problems.

We want to get married. No one will ever know how many

thousands of delayed marriages among Negro youth have been caused by the depression. The result in many cases has been a distressing demoralization and an increase in the prevalence of venereal diseases. Our only real hope for a solution lies in marriage and homemaking, in sex education, made available in our schools.

We want an opportunity to develop our talents. We are eager and anxious to contribute to the Negro's cultural heritage as artists, musicians, writers and actors. At present our opportunity for expression is severely limited. We realize that most of us do not possess the ability of a Paul Robeson or a Marian Anderson, but we do feel that if allowed the opportunity, we could make original contributions to science, the arts, drama, literature and music.

For these reasons we support the Federal Arts bill designed to open new fields for young people whose major interests are along cultural lines. And admitting that the passage of this bill is only an eventual possibility and by no means a certainty, we have decided to take upon ourselves the establishment of Negro community theatres in cities throughout the South.

We want a religious life. This may seem a bit surprising in view of the prevailing opinion that Negro youth has become increasingly irreligious day by day, but it is none the less true. We cherish the religious heritage of our people and the contribution that has been made through the church to our advancement. The significant feature of our idea of religion is that we insist upon a stricter application of Christian principles to everyday life. We refuse lip service to the ideal of brotherhood when in practice that ideal is consistently disregarded. We want the church to help us meet concrete life situations.

What must the church do to give us the type of meaningful religious experience we seek? We feel that it must first identify itself with the masses of crucified people of the South. It must become the center of community life, organizing within itself youth and adult groups for Christian social action and promoting fellowship by interdenominational and interracial cooperation.

We want a world at peace. We look with grave concern upon the growth of fascism and the fascist threat to peace because of the inherent danger of raising the racial myth to a place of major concern in world policies. As a means of obtaining peace we feel that the only workable solution yet proposed is the quarantine of aggressors suggested by the President in his speech of last October 5.

These then, are the aspirations of Southern Negro youth: we want the right to vote, to work and to complete our education; the opportunity to marry; the chance to express ourselves; the privilege of a satisfactory religious life, and the assurance of a peaceful world.

In short, we want to live!

From *Opportunity,* May, 1938.

In the same year that Franklin
D. Roosevelt entered the White House, Adolf Hitler became
the dictator of Germany. Mussolini had been in power in Italy
for a decade, and Japan had already seized Manchuria. In
1935 Mussolini invaded Ethiopia, and Negroes were among
the first Americans to protest and to call for international
action to halt aggression by the fascist power. Negroes knew
what the doctrine of racial supremacy meant; they did not
have to wait for Hitler to murder millions to find out. But the
democracies took no concerted action to halt the rise of fascism and Hitler easily overthrew Austria and took over Czech-
oslovakia. In 1939 he rolled over Poland, and Europe was

pitched into another world war. America soon began to prepare for what seemed inevitable involvement, building up a large fighting force and making the guns and ships and planes and tanks and ammunition that would be needed.

The armed forces were segregated at that time, and discrimination was common. In the war industries, too, the barriers were up. Negroes had great trouble getting jobs. Federal officials spoke out against discrimination but industry was deaf. Janitors? Sweepers? Yes, those jobs were available. But aircraft mechanics? Welders? No, the corporations said, not for black labor.

What have we to fight for, asked many Negroes. Even Negro leaders known to be conservative, those who thought things were gradually changing for the better, showed open rebellion. Many Americans, they pointed out, were acting as though the war against Hitlerism was not nearly so important as preventing Negroes from winning some democracy for themselves.

In November 1941, only a month before the Japanese attack on Pearl Harbor plunged America into the war against fascism on two fronts, Roi Ottley, a Negro journalist, surveyed the Negro press to see what it reflected of the mood in the black ghettoes.

Hitlerism at home . . .

1941

THROUGHOUT THE urban areas of the country, the Negro communities are seething with resentment. . . . This unrest has recently been brought to a head by twin factors which have come to the surface in the national emergency but whose roots lie deep in American life: the treatment of Negro members of the army and the frustration Negroes feel at being barred from jobs in defense industries.

Negro newspapers describe the army situation as bad indeed. They cite as examples, race riots at Fort Oswego; fighting at Camp Davis; discrimination at Fort Devens; jim-crow conditions at Camps Blanding and Lee; stabbings at Fort Huachuca; killings at Fort Bragg; and the edict "not to shake a nigger's hand" at Camp Upton.

Nearly every day there are reports of Negroes going AWOL, particularly those stationed in Southern camps. . . . Following friction with the white population, forty-three Negroes of the Ninety-fourth Engineers (labor) Battalion from Chicago and Detroit departed from the maneuver area near

Gurdon, Arkansas. In explaining the "racial difficulties" involved, Major Gen. Robert C. Richardson Jr., white, said that ". . . some of these Northern Negroes, not understanding the attitude of the Southerner, and apparently to avoid further trouble, left their command."

This is too pat an answer. It ignores the undercurrent of feeling among all Negroes that comes to the surface at the least provocation; and it slides over the fact that the Northern Negro knows the Southern viewpoint all too well. A Negro who has lived in the freer atmosphere of the North and becomes aware of his political rights will not relinquish them or put up with abuse because he happens to be in the South. That he wears the uniform of the United States Army increases his self-respect.

To some Southerners such a man is a dangerous "nigger" who must be made to "know his place"—with violence and terror, if necessary. The prejudiced Southerner refuses to accord even the ordinary decencies to the Negro—uniform or no uniform—and is not impressed by the statements of administration leaders about extending democracy to the oppressed. In his view, democracy is not a way of life for all, but a luxury for better-class white people only.

The sharply differing views of the Northern Negro and the prejudiced white Southerner are now meeting head-on. This was revealed in the flare-up at Fort Bragg, North Carolina, the result of an affray in which a Negro soldier and a white military policeman were killed. In this instance, however, the killing of the white MP was the act of a Southern Negro whose resentment against injustice mounted to a desperate thrust for human dignity.

According to the best available accounts, this soldier, Ned Turman, voiced objections to an attack on a fellow Negro soldier and was cracked over the head with a club by a white MP. In wrestling to protect himself, the Negro managed to snatch his assailant's gun. Brandishing it, he stepped back and cried: "I'm going to break up you MP's beating us colored soldiers!" And with that, he fired the fatal shot. He was immediately shot to death by another white MP, who also had participated in the fracas. After the shooting, whole companies not involved in the affair—their Negro officers included—were forced to stand all night with their hands above their heads while armed military policemen patrolled the camp.

The daily newspapers . . . maintained a silence that made the situation no less real. Few were the voices of white people protesting against such treatment of members of the country's army. Similar acts committed by Nazis outrage American opinion and result in columns and columns of newspaper comment.

Negroes, however, were outspoken about the affair to the point of being inflammatory. George S. Schuyler, a well know commentator who has few illusions about his race and its problems, spoke of the "racial hatred, official cowardice and hypocrisy" rampant in the "new so-called people's army," and held that "every American, whose soul was not corroded by Negrophobia, should be enraged." After condemning "Hitlerism at Home," The Pittsburgh *Courier,* largest-selling Negro newspaper in the country, went on to say editorially that "Nothing short of the most drastic punishment of officers and enlisted men among the white military police will satisfy a justifiably aroused Negro people."

The equally influential Baltimore *Afro-American,* in calling for mass action, observed that "One individual marching up and down Pennsylvania Avenue in front of the White House denouncing race prejudice is arrested as a crank. Ten thousand persons get respectful attention. When great batches of drafted men desert rather than serve in the army down in Dixie, the War Department will then do something."

In a typical letter to the editor, a Negro man-in-the-street wrote: "When I read these things I am forced to wonder just how far removed is this brand of democracy that we practice from fascism, Nazism and barbarism. . . . Lest someone chide me for not being loyal, may I say that I am as loyal as America permits me to be."

"Negroes have been patient, loyal and patriotic," the *Amsterdam-Star News* remarked editorially, "but they will not be destroyed!"

From *New Republic,* November 10, 1941.

P*rivate pleas and peaceful peti-*
tions changed nobody's mind. The industrialists, the generals,
and the politicians went on doing their Jim Crow dance. Negro
leaders saw that powerful, mass action was needed. In Jan-
uary 1941, A. Philip Randolph, the head of the Brotherhood
of Sleeping Car Porters, proposed a March on Washington to
demand that government do something. Soon all the heads of
the major Negro organizations had joined in; the movement
had the mass support of Negroes everywhere. Washington was
alarmed at signs of revolt in time of crisis. The President and
others tried to have the march called off but the leaders re-
fused. As the planned day came in sight and marchers were

preparing to board trains for the capital, President Roosevelt told Randolph that it was not necessary to march; he would take the action desired.

On June 25, 1941, the President issued Executive Order 8802, banning discrimination in defense industries or in government "because of race, creed, color, or national origin." A Fair Employment Practices Commission was set up to carry out the order and the government began its first programs to better the economic position of the Negro.

It was a great beginning, but only that. There was much more to be done, and the need for continuous pressure was great. The tactic of nonviolent, mass resistance to injustice had proved its value, and in the years to come it would be used far more widely, from the little towns of the South to the giant cities of the North. In 1942 Randolph spelled out the program of the March on Washington movement to continue the fight against Hitlerism abroad and for full democracy at home.

March on Washington . . .

1942

1. WE DEMAND, in the interest of national unity, the abrogation of every law which makes a distinction in treatment between citizens based on religion, creed, color or national origin. This means an end to Jim Crow in education, in housing, in transportation and in every other social, economic and political privilege; and especially, we demand, in the capital of the nation, an end to all segregation in public places and in public institutions.

2. We demand legislation to enforce the Fifth and Fourteenth Amendments guaranteeing that no person shall be deprived of life, liberty or property without due process of law, so that the full weight of the national government may be used for the protection of life and thereby may end the disgrace of lynching.

3. We demand the enforcement of the Fourteenth and Fifteenth Amendments and the enactment of the Pepper Poll-Tax bill so that all barriers in the exercise of the suffrage are eliminated.

4. We demand the abolition of segregation and discrimination in the Army, Navy, Marine Corps, Air Corps and all other branches of national defense.

5. We demand an end to discrimination in jobs and job training. Further, we demand that the FEPC be made a permanent administrative agency of the U.S. Government and that it be given power to enforce its decisions based on its findings.

6. We demand that federal funds be withheld from any agency which practices discrimination in the use of such funds.

7. We demand colored and minority group representation on all administrative agencies so that these groups may have recognition of their democratic right to participate in formulating policies.

8. We demand representation for the colored and minority racial groups on all missions, political and technical, which will be sent to the peace conference so that the interests of all people everywhere may be fully recognized and justly provided for in the postwar settlement.

From *Survey,* November, 1942.

CARL T. ROWAN

C*arl T. Rowan was born in Tennessee in 1925. He spent most of his first 18 years in Mc-Minnville, a town of about 5,000 in middle Tennessee, at the foot of the Cumberlands. World War II took him out of a life of almost complete segregation. After service in the Navy, he was educated at Oberlin College and the University of Minnesota's journalism school. His superb reporting for the Minneapolis* Morning Tribune *(he was one of the first Negroes to work on a white newspaper) earned him national recognition and many honors. Soon he was contributing to leading national periodicals. He was appointed by President Kennedy to be ambassador to Finland; and later he served under President*

166

Johnson as director of the United States Information Agency.

In his book South of Freedom, *Rowan reported on a 6,000 mile tour in which he crisscrossed his native South to try to strike a balance sheet of American race relations. In an early chapter he goes back to the Tennessee town of his childhood and compares it with the McMinnville he grew up in.*

A good town . . .

1951

I RETURNED TO McMinnville, to
the familiar gravel streets that I had walked for almost two
decades. I returned to frame houses with decaying foundations, to yards barren of grass; and even the tiniest hovel with
the farthest-away privy had its nostalgic meaning. Some were
houses where human beings—people I knew—lived like rats,
and where rats outnumbered the people. Some were houses I
knew by the starred flags of World War II, which still hung
dusty in windows. They were houses where my schoolmates
lived, or once had lived. . . .

I went to a dumpy little cafe that townspeople call "The
Slobbery Rock." That name aptly describes the shaky old
structure, which sits on a rocky ledge just two blocks from the
heart of downtown. A juxebox blared out a blues tune. High-
school youngsters of fourteen to sixteen, and a drunken woman
of at least fifty-five, dragged across the sawdust-strewn dance
floor. The air was thick with greasy smoke, heavy with the
mingled odors of laborers and school-girl perfumes. There, at

The Slobbery Rock, gathered ninety-nine per cent of Negro McMinnville's youth, out for their weekend entertainment. . . .

When I was a youth, Negro youngsters had two choices for away-from-home entertainment. They went to one of the two segregated movies, where they sat in a balcony not even provided with a restroom; then they either went home or to "The Rock." It takes no sociologist to guess which course they usually chose. McMinnville did have one other Negro cafe, but it was too small for dancing and usually closed very early. There was a skating rink—barred to Negroes. There was a tax-supported swimming pool—barred to Negroes. . . .

The McMinnville of 1951 was little different, I found. "The Rock" was still "the place to go." There was one new place, Harvey's Bar B-Q Stand. Harvey's was clean and the food delicious, but a resentful Negro community talked of boycotting it because the place, run by Harvey Faulkner, a Negro, was segregated. Negro youngsters complained that when they asked for straws in their soft drinks they were told none was available. On the other side of Harvey's, however, whites sipped through straws.

"Worst insult of all," said a Negro teacher, "are the signs put up on the colored side: NO DRINKING, NO CURSING, NO MATCHING." Faulkner had put up no such signs on the white side.

I asked Faulkner why he ran a Jim Crow place. Most cafes run by whites bar Negroes entirely, a few allowing them to enter by the back door for food to take out. A Negro ordering hamburgers at the Serv-All (sic) must stand on the street and wait until they are cooked. Harvey Faulkner knew all this as well as I. He leaned on the counter, studying my question; then, as if the answer had popped out of nowhere, snapped: "I've got to live; white folks represent nearly half my trade."

What McMinnvillian could condemn Faulkner? He had set no precedent; Negro McMinnville had done that in many ways. Had not Bernard High School annually set aside front seats for white guests who came to see our closing-of-school plays? Had not the Church of Christ reserved many of the front seats for whites who came to its tent revival? I stood in Harvey's, on the colored side, peeking around the counter into the white side, and I realized that his Jim Crow establishment was just another sacrifice offered up to the Southland's deity, segregation. Faulkner, like myself and millions of other Negroes, had made concessions to Jim Crow in adjusting his life to the South's double standard. The signs on the colored side of Harvey's were a manifestation of that double standard. In a few misty seconds, I seemed to recall countless incidents in my relatively short lifetime that were manifestations of that double standard.

Against this background, I could understand Faulkner's decision, even if I could not justify it. He had learned the who, what, when, where, and why of the South the same way I had, and the nucleus of every lesson was strict compliance with the mores of the particular community; above this there was neither justice nor common sense. That made running a cafe something like going home from school—the way I went home from school in the early thirties. You learned to put up a partition so white and black hands never lifted a glass from the same counter, though it be the same piece of wood, and you learned the same way I learned the ABC's of Dixie race relations: words like nigger, redneck, darky, peckerwood, shine, cracker, eight-ball, snowflake, and any combination of these with bastard or sonofabitch. The way I learned them, these were third-grade words.

McMinnville's Negro school was located in such a way that a group of white children had to pass it on their way home from their school. They met homebound Negro children, and each afternoon there would come the chant:

"Eeny, meeny, miny, mo; catch a nigger by the toe . . ."

And a Negro youngster would reply:

"We've got cheese at home; all I need is a cracker to go with it. . . ."

Since no group could clearly establish dominance by hurling epithets, the issue was resolved into who should use the sidewalks, and the conflict assumed physical proportions. Young fists, propelled by hatreds of past generations, hatreds no youngster could give reason for, would fly at young faces of opposite color, churning blood from noses and feeding grist to the mills of hatred for another generation. But this could not go on indefinitely—not in McMinnville. White parents apparently complained to the school superintendent, who called the Negro principal. Soon, a swollen lip betraying me as a participant in the strife, I stood before the Negro principal with several schoolmates.

With the wisdom of a man who has been burned, lecturing children against playing with fire, the principal explained that we could not win. "If the whites want the sidewalks, get off. Walk in the street," he ordered. With those words, words I dislike to remember, "peace" came to McMinnville to the extent that nobody fought over sidewalks. This was because a few youngsters walked in the street; the indomitable among us climbed fences and went home across fields rather than face the youngsters for whom we had had to give up the sidewalks. Twenty years' time has enabled McMinnville to decide that, though in passing they need not nod the "Good morning" that is typical of that small Southern town, whites and blacks may share the sidewalks. "Peace" remains with McMinnville in that sense.

It is this capacity for change that has made McMinnville a "good Southern town," in the words of her Negro citizens. They mean that for a quarter century there have been no lynchings, no race riots. Policemen do not "pick on" Negro neighborhoods. There are no Ku Klux Klan pogroms, no bigots shouting in the streets that all Negroes must be shipped to Africa. In that negative sense—because it is better than a lot of small Southern communities—McMinnville is a "good town."

But McMinnville is a peaceful town, I found in 1951, because, in the words of a former river-buddy, "no Negro in his right mind" would show up at the city swimming-pool with trunks and the intention of swimming. And McMinnville Negroes still do not go to the tax-supported public library, ask for a book, and sit down and read. If Negro pupils want books, their teachers must go get the books and bring them out to the pupils. Skating is still something Negroes do on sidewalks or not at all. And when a street is blocked off for square dancing, Negroes watch from a distance.

From *South of Freedom,* by Carl T. Rowan, Knopf, 1952.

MARTIN LUTHER KING, JR.

A *"good" Southern town was a peaceful town, peaceful because no Negro challenged the system of segregation and discrimination. The peace—never universal, always only on the surface—was soon broken. Step by step through the 1930s and 1940s the NAACP had carried the fight for the franchise and for equal educational opportunities through the courts. On May 17, 1954, came the sweeping decision by the U.S. Supreme Court that persons "required on the basis of race to attend separate schools were deprived of the equal protection of the laws guaranteed by the Fourteenth Amendment." Racial segregation in the public schools was* outlawed. The "separate but equal" doctrine the Court had upheld in 1896 was set aside.

There was jubilation at first. Millions of Negroes rejoiced that at last—over 90 years after Emancipation—the basic rights of democracy for all were recognized. But soon resistance to the Court's ruling developed. The battle for school desegregation became international news. Clinton, Nashville, Atlanta, Little Rock, Oxford—the names flashed across the world's front pages. Refusal to comply with the law ranged from simple inaction or token integration to riots and bombings.

The pace of school desegregation was agonizingly slow. Ten years after the Court's decision only 9.2 per cent of the Negro public school students in the Southern and border states were attending desegregated classes. (At that rate it would take a hundred years to complete the process.) And wherever Negroes sought to exercise the basic right of the ballot, or the right to live in homes in whatever neighborhood they chose, intimidation and violence met them. In the realms of law and morality victories had been won, but everyday life had become a battleground of gunpowder and dynamite, cross-burnings and beatings, arson and murder.

Against the violent direct action of the white citizens councils and the Klan a new technique came into being. Negroes decided to take matters into their own hands. Nonviolent direct action, a form of mass, passive resistance, emerged as the means of advancing the struggle for civil rights. Montgomery, Alabama, the cradle of the Confederacy, was the scene. The rulers of that city of "genteel" segregation, with a population almost equally divided between white and Negro, had long *believed in the right of whites to be master and Negroes to be servant. Their contentment with things as they were was shattered the day that courageous Mrs. Rosa Parks refused to move to the Jim Crow section of the bus. The story of Mrs. Parks and the great Montgomery bus boycott of 1955-1956 is told by Rev. Martin Luther King, Jr., who led the protest movement. Here he not only describes what happened but explains how, during the long siege, his own thinking was shaped along paths marked out by Thoreau and Gandhi.*

In the end, the Montgomery Negroes won their battle, and the boycott was picked up throughout the country as the weapon that could force change. Dr. King in 1964 was awarded the Nobel Prize for peace in recognition of his championship of the nonviolence precept.

Bus boycott . . .

1954

ON DECEMBER 1, 1955, an attractive Negro seamstress, Mrs. Rosa Parks, boarded the Cleveland Avenue bus in downtown Montgomery. She was returning home after her regular day's work in Montgomery Fair—a leading department store. Tired from long hours on her feet, Mrs. Parks sat down in the first seat behind the section reserved for whites. Not long after she took her seat, the bus operator ordered her, along with three other Negro passengers, to move back in order to accommodate boarding white passengers. By this time every seat in the bus was taken. This meant that if Mrs. Parks followed the driver's command she would have to stand while a white male passenger, who had just boarded the bus, would sit. The other three Negro passengers immediately complied with the driver's request. But Mrs. Parks quietly refused. The result was her arrest.

There was to be much speculation about why Mrs. Parks did not obey the driver. Many people in the white community argued that she had been "planted" by the NAACP in order to lay the groundwork for a test case. . . .

But the accusation was totally unwarranted, as the testimony of both Mrs. Parks and the officials of the NAACP revealed. . . . Mrs. Parks' refusal to move back was her intrepid affirmation that she had had enough. It was an individual expression of a timeless longing for human dignity and freedom. She was not "planted" there by the NAACP, or any other organization; she was planted there by her personal sense of dignity and self-respect. . . .

Only E. D. Nixon—the signer of Mrs. Parks's bond—and one or two other persons were aware of the arrest when it occurred early Thursday evening. Later in the evening the word got around to a few influential women of the community, mostly members of the Women's Political Council. After a series of telephone calls back and forth they agreed that the Negroes should boycott the buses. They immediately suggested the idea to Nixon, and he readily concurred. In his usual courageous manner he agreed to spearhead the idea.

Early Friday morning, December 2, Nixon called me. He was so caught up in what he was about to say that he forgot to greet me with the usual "hello" but plunged immediately into the story of what had happened to Mrs. Parks the night before. I listened, deeply shocked, as he described the humiliating incident. "We have taken this type of thing too long already," Nixon concluded, his voice trembling. "I feel that the time has come to boycott the buses. Only through a boycott can we make it clear to the white folks that we will not accept this type of treatment any longer."

I agreed at once that some protest was necessary, and that the boycott method would be an effective one.

Just before calling me Nixon had discussed the idea with Rev. Ralph Abernathy, the young minister of Montgomery's First Baptist Church, who was to become one of the central figures in the protest, and one of my closest associates. Abernathy also felt a bus boycott was our best course of action. So for thirty or forty minutes the three of us telephoned back and forth concerning plans and strategy. Nixon suggested that we call a meeting of all the ministers and civic leaders the same evening in order to get their thinking on the proposal, and I offered my church as the meeting place. The three of us got busy immediately. With the sanction of Rev. H. H. Hubbard—president of the Baptist Ministerial Alliance—Abernathy and I began calling all of the Baptist ministers. Since most of the Methodist ministers were attending a denominational meeting in one of the local churches that afternoon, it was possible for Abernathy to get the announcement to all of them simultaneously. . . .

By early afternoon the arrest of Mrs. Parks was becoming public knowledge. Word of it spread around the community like uncontrolled fire. Telephones began to ring in almost rhythmic succession. By two o'clock an enthusiastic group had mimeographed leaflets concerning the arrest and the proposed boycott, and by evening these had been widely circulated.

As the hour for the evening meeting arrived, I approached the doors of the church with some apprehension, wondering how many of the leaders would respond to our call. Fortunately, it was one of those pleasant winter nights of unseasonable warmth, and to our relief, almost everybody who had been invited was on hand. More than forty people, from every segment of Negro life, were crowded into the large church meeting room. I saw physicians, schoolteachers, lawyers, businessmen, postal workers, union leaders, and clergymen. Virtually every organization of the Negro community was represented. . . .

Bennett moved into action, explaining the purpose of the gathering. With excited gestures he reported on Mrs. Parks's resistance and her arrest. He presented the proposal that the Negro citizens of Montgomery should boycott the buses on Monday in protest. "Now is the time to move," he concluded. "This is no time to talk; it is time to act." . . .

Immediately questions began to spring up from the floor. . . . How long would the protest last? How would the idea be further disseminated throughout the community? How would the people be transported to and from their jobs? . . .

Not once did anyone question the validity or desirability of the boycott itself. It seemed to be the unanimous sense of the group that the boycott should take place.

The ministers endorsed the plan with enthusiasm, and promised to go to their congregations on Sunday morning and drive home their approval of the projected one-day protest. Their cooperation was significant, since virtually all of the influential Negro ministers of the city were present. It was decided that we should hold a citywide mass meeting on Monday night, December 5, to determine how long we would abstain from riding the buses. . . .

The group agreed that additional leaflets should be distributed on Saturday, and the chairman appointed a committee, including myself, to prepare the statement. . . . It read as follows:

> Don't ride the bus to work, to town, to school, or any place Monday, December 5.
>
> Another Negro woman has been arrested and put in jail because she refused to give up her bus seat.
>
> Don't ride the buses to work, to town, to school, or anywhere on Monday. If you work, take a cab, or share a ride, or walk.
>
> Come to a mass meeting, Monday at 7:00 P.M., at the Holt Street Baptist Church for further instruction.

The final question before the meeting concerned transportation. It was agreed that we should try to get the Negro taxi companies of the city—eighteen in number, with approximately 210 taxis—to transport the people for the same price that they were currently paying on the bus.

With these responsibilities before us the meeting closed. We left with our hearts caught up in a great idea. The hours were moving fast. The clock on the wall read almost midnight, but the clock in our souls revealed that it was daybreak.

I was so excited that I slept very little that night, and early next morning I was on my way to the church to get the leaflets out. By nine o'clock the church secretary had finished mimeographing the 7,000 leaflets and by eleven o'clock an army of women and young people had taken them off to distribute by hand.

Those on the committee that was to contact the taxi companies got to work early Saturday afternoon. They worked assiduously, and by evening they had reached practically all of the companies, and triumphantly reported that every one of them so far had agreed to cooperate with the proposed boycott by transporting the passengers to and from work for the regular ten-cent bus fare.

Meanwhile our efforts to get the word across to the Negro community were abetted in an unexpected way, A maid who could not read very well came into possession of one of the unsigned appeals that had been distributed Friday afternoon. Apparently not knowing what the leaflet said, she gave it to her employer. As soon as the white employer received the notice she turned it over to the local newspaper, and the Montgomery *Advertiser* made the contents of the leaflet a front-page story on Saturday morning. It appears that the *Advertiser* printed the story in order to let the white community know what the Negroes were up to; but the whole thing turned out to the Negroes' advantage, since it served to bring the information to hundreds who had not previously heard of the plan. By Sunday afternoon word had spread to practically every Negro citizen of Montgomery. Only a few people who lived in remote areas had not heard of it.

After a heavy day of work, I went home late Sunday afternoon and sat down to read the morning paper. There was a long article on the proposed boycott. Implicit throughout the article, I noticed, was the idea that the Negroes were preparing to use the same approach to their problem as the White Citizens Councils used. This suggested parallel had serious implications. The White Citizens Councils had had their birth in Mississippi a few months after the Supreme Court's school decision had come into being to preserve segregation. The Councils had multiplied rapidly throughout the South, purporting to achieve their ends by the legal maneuvers of "interposition" and "nullification." Unfortunately, however, the actions of some of these Councils extended far beyond the bounds of the law. Their methods were the methods of open and covert terror, brutal intimidation, and threats of starvation to Negro men, women, and children. They took open economic reprisals against whites who dared to protest their defiance of the law, and the aim of their boycotts was not merely to impress their victims but to destroy them if possible.

Disturbed by the fact that our pending action was being equated with the boycott methods of the White Citizens Councils, I was forced for the first time to think seriously on the nature of the boycott. Up to this time I had uncritically accepted this method as our best course of action. Now certain doubts began to bother me. Were we following an ethical course of action? Is the boycott method basically unchristian? Isn't it a negative approach to the solution of a problem? Is it true that we would be following the course of some of the White Citizens Councils? Even if lasting practical results came from such a boycott, would immoral means justify moral ends? Each of these questions demanded honest answers.

I had to recognize that the boycott method could be used to unethical and unchristian ends. I had to concede, further, that this was the method used so often by the White Citizens Councils to deprive many Negroes, as well as white persons of good will, of the basic necessities of life. But certainly, I said to myself, our pending actions could not be interpreted in this light. Our purposes were altogether different. We would use this method to give birth to justice and freedom, and also to urge men to comply with the law of the land; the White Citizens Councils used it to perpetuate the reign of injustice and human servitude, and urged men to defy the law of the land. I reasoned, therefore, that the word "boycott" was really a misnomer for our proposed action. A boycott suggests an economic squeeze, leaving one bogged down in a negative. But we were concerned with the positive. Our concern would not be to put the bus company out of business, but to put justice in business.

As I thought further I came to see that what we were really doing was withdrawing our cooperation from an evil system, rather than merely withdrawing our economic support from the bus company. The bus company, being an external expression of the system, would naturally suffer, but the basic aim was to refuse to cooperate with evil. At this point I began to think about Thoreau's Essay on Civil Disobedience. I remembered how, as a college student, I had been moved when I first read this work. I became convinced that what we were preparing to do in Montgomery was related to what Thoreau had expressed. We were simply saying to the white community, "We can no longer lend our cooperation to an evil system."

Something began to say to me, "He who passively accepts evil is as much involved in it as he who helps to perpetrate it. He who accepts evil without protesting against it is really cooperating with it." When oppressed people willingly accept their oppression they only serve to give the oppressor a convenient justification for his acts. Often the oppressor goes along unaware of the evil involved in his oppression so long as the oppressed accepts it. So in order to be true to one's conscience and true to God, a righteous man has no alternative but to refuse to cooperate with an evil system. This I felt was the nature of our action. From this moment on I conceived of our movement as an act of massive noncooperation. . . .

From *Stride Toward Freedom,* by Martin Luther King, Jr., Harper, 1958.

T*hree times Martin Luther King's home was shot up or bombed during the Montgomery bus boycott, but in the end the city's Negroes carried the banner of nonviolence to victory. Montgomery was a turning point. It meant new times had come. New leaders came out of that long trial, young men and women native to the South, helped by but not dependent upon remote Northern friends. As the U.S. Supreme Court ruled against segregated buses, and went on with ban after ban against Jim Crow, Negroes were affirmed in their deep feeling that they were right in their protest, that direct action could produce the social change justice demanded. They had won strength through struggle.*

Another chapter opened early in 1960, when Negro college students in Greensboro, N.C., sat down at a lunch counter in Woolworth's and vowed that they and others would stay there until Negroes were served. The sit-ins won national attention, and swiftly other students were sitting at other lunch counters, risking everything to show they wanted to be treated as human beings.

In six months that first Woolworth's was open to all races. By the year's end Negroes were being served at hundreds of other stores, and in the years that followed sit-ins brought desegregation to movie theatres, amusement parks, beaches, swimming pools, hotels. In the spring of 1961 the movement spread to transportation. Freedom riders attacked segregation in buses and waiting rooms and met savage resistance that ended only when federal marshals by the hundreds appeared. The disorders brought the Interstate Commerce Commission to outlaw segregation in all trains and buses and terminals.

The tactics of Southern resistance changed. Instead of arresting demonstrators for violating segregation ordinances the local officials flung them into jail for disorderly conduct or for creating disturbances. The cases had to go to the courts, taking years on appeal and costing heavily for bonds.

But direct action continued. It won victories in some places; it failed in others; but it succeeded in applying the vast pressure needed to obtain the passage of a new federal Civil Rights Act which put the immediate goals of the movement into law.

What the bus boycotters and the students had begun proved the Negro's courage. He risked his job, his education, and his life in the fight for first-class citizenship. He learned as he struggled, and the struggle renewed his will to struggle. He saw him-

self in a new light and he made millions of whites the world over open their eyes to the new reality.

The document that follows is testimony from one young Negro on the Southern battle lines. It is from Terrell County in Georgia, where Sheriff Zeke Mathews said in 1962, "We want our colored people to go on living like they have for the last hundred years." The sheriff, 20 years in office without opposition, liked things the way they were. With 8,209 Negroes and only 4,553 whites, the voters' registration rolls showed only 51 Negroes as against 2,894 whites. The Student Nonviolent Coordinating Committee (SNCC) put field secretaries in the county to work on a voter registration drive. Charlie H. Wingfield, Jr. was one of the local Negroes who wanted to register to vote.

Oh brothers,
if you only knew . . .
1960s

THERE WAS NINE of us kids in the family and we all had to work a lot. I flunked two grades in school because of the unjust system we had to live under. I stayed out of school a lot of days because I couldn't let my mother go to the cotton field and try to support all of us. I had to decide which was more important, getting an education or letting my mother suffer along. When my father stopped working I had to stay out of school more than ever before. I picked cotton and pecans for two cents a pound. I went to the fields six in the morning and worked until seven in the afternoon. When it came time to weigh up so to speak, my heart, body and bones would be aching, burning and trembling. I stood there and stared the white men right in their eyes while they cheated me, other members of my family, and the rest of the Negroes that were working. They had their weighing scales loaded with lead and the rod would always be pointing toward the sky. There were times when I wanted to speak but my fearful mother would always tell me to keep silent. The sun was awful hot and the days were long. It was like being baked in an oven. When I went to bed at night I could see bolls of cotton staring me right in the face.

I would look at my sisters and my heart would say . . . dear sisters, I wish you could have and enjoy some of the finer things that life has to offer. I would look at my brothers and my heart would cry . . . oh brothers, if you only knew what it's like to live and enjoy life, instead of working like bees all the time to stay alive. Then I would look at my parents and my heart would utter . . . some day I'll build you a castle and you never have to bend your backs in another field. Last and least I would think of myself. I wished I had enough money to help the poor, build a playing center and a new church for our community. All these wonderful thoughts made me forget about my sorrow troubles but as I stop day dreaming I would be the saddest guy in the whole world.

My hands are like a history book. They tell a countless number of sad sad stories. Like a flowing river they seem to have no end. The cost of survival was high. Why I paid it I will never know.

I got expelled from the Lee County Training School for asking for some equipment for our school. All of the facilities that I asked was necessary for the proper kind of education a student needs. The officials of the city refused to let me register to vote. They also notified the surrounding schools not to let me enroll. I went to Shreveport, La., the 29th of September. I attended the Wash. High School there for two weeks. I was really enjoying myself and I was learning an awful lot of things that I had never heard of before. The standards of the school is one of the higher that can be found in the U.S. I talked with the F.B.I.'s and shortly afterward white people started riding by the house. They started calling the lady that I was living with hanging the phone up once she answered it. She told me that she didn't want her home bombed and I had to leave.

Statement to Student Nonviolent Coordinating Committee,
by Charlie H. Wingfield, Jr., Terrell County, Ga.

MRS. FANNIE LOU HAMER
AT THE DEMOCRATIC NATIONAL CONVENTION, 1964

"*The right of citizens of the United States to vote shall not be denied or abridged by the United States or by any State on account of race, color, or previous condition of servitude.*"

191

So runs the Fifteenth Amendment, written into the United States Constitution in the year 1870. The words are simple and direct, but they have not been understood or respected in the South for about a hundred years. When Reconstruction was overthrown, the right to vote was gradually cut down until by the last years of the nineteenth century the Fifteenth Amendment was only a paper promise. First there was the poll tax, pioneered by Mississippi; then the requirement that voters be able to understand and interpret the state constitution, again a Mississippi innovation; and then the grandfather clause, which let only those vote without tests who had a forebear who had voted in 1866 or earlier. Everyone else—meaning all Negroes—had to submit to stiff educational tests.

Some Negroes did vote in the South, even in Mississippi, for several decades after the Civil War. (Around 1900 about 9 per cent of the state's voting-age Negroes were still on Mississippi's rolls.) In the next decades the Supreme Court struck down one after another of the unconstitutional barriers to the ballot, but in a large part of the South it made no difference. Negroes still were not allowed to vote. In 1964 only 5 percent of the Negroes in Mississippi were registered. In many counties almost every white was on the voting rolls but not one Negro. White supremacy had ruled for generations, and it did not mean to give up or share its power. The methods used to keep Negroes from voting were not subtle. They were crude and trivial at one end, but brutal, inhuman, even murderous, at the other end.

Trying hard on their own to win the ballot, Southern Negroes could make little progress against the economic and political power of the white supremacists. The Civil Rights Act of 1957 allowed the Justice Department to challenge voting discrimination. Now the federal government could no longer say it was without power to enforce respect for the right to vote. But the years that followed saw only the smallest change. The national government did not succeed in establishing the rule of the Constitution in the deep South. Some said it was because Washington was not really trying. The Southern police and local and state officials made their own law, with no regard for the Constitution, and the federal government too often continued to act as though it were powerless.

The record is full of crimes of violence, committed by Southern police against United States citizens. The times when citizens have been denied equal protection of the laws and of freedom of speech and assembly, are innumerable. Every such instance is a violation of the Civil Rights Enforcement Act of 1870, but in only a few cases did the Justice Department intervene.

In 1960, Mississippi began to move toward a new day. It started with a meeting between Robert Parris Moses, a young Harlem Negro with a master's degree from Harvard, and Alonzo Moore, a farmer from Cleveland, Mississippi, who was head of the local NAACP. They planned a campaign to register Negroes to vote. The first voter registration school opened in one county the next summer, staffed by SNCC workers. Negroes went down to the county seat to register, and some of them passed the test. The news raced to other counties, and there too schools soon opened. Beatings, arrests, jailings, heavy bail bonds were used to halt the movement. One Negro farmer was murdered the next month and a Negro witness to the killing was later shot to death. But the voter registration drive went on, side by side with sit-ins, marches, and freedom rides. In 1962 a bigger plan was drawn for a unified voter registration program. The NAACP, CORE, SCLC, and SNCC shared the funds contributed by foundations for the new Voter Education Project.

Thousands of Negroes in Mississippi were reached by the movement. In 1964, it expanded to a special civil rights program undertaken for the summer months. Its aim was a massive education, community improvement, and voter registration drive. Under the leadership of several groups combined in a Council of Federated Organizations (COFO), students, lawyers, doctors, teachers, and clergymen volunteered their time and talents for a peaceful, nonviolent campaign.

Mississippi officials instantly countered the announcement with plans for resistance. New local and state laws were adopted to further limit peaceful assembly and free speech and to hamper the work of the freedom schools and community centers.

To call public attention to the Mississippi summer project, a group of private citizens concerned with civil rights held unofficial hearings on Mississippi in Washington on June 8, 1964. The panel took the testimony of many witnesses from the state, testimony later entered in the Congressional Record. *Among the witnesses was Fannie Lou Hamer. Mrs. Hamer, then 47, was one of a family of 20 children. Married, she was herself the mother of two, and had worked all her life as a sharecropper in Ruleville. She went down to register after she heard SNCC workers talk at a mass meeting in her church. Later, when she was evicted from the plantation where she had worked as a timekeeper and sharecropper for 18 years, she became a field secretary for SNCC. She also became one of the three Negroes to campaign for Congress in 1964 on the Mississippi Freedom Democratic Party ticket.*

Tell about Mississippi . . .

1964

Q. Would you state your name and address, please?

A. My name is Fannie Lou Hamer, and I exist at 626 East Lafayette Street in Ruleville, Miss.

Q. Mrs. Hamer, what is it that brings you before the panel today?

A. To tell about some of the brutality in the State of Mississippi. I will begin from the first beginning, August 31, in 1962.

I traveled 26 miles to the county courthouse to try to register to become a first-class citizen. I was fired the 31st of August in 1962 from a plantation where I had worked as a time-keeper and a sharecropper for 18 years. My husband had worked there 30 years.

I was met by my children when I returned from the courthouse, and my girl and my husband's cousin told me that this man my husband worked for was raising a lot of Cain. I went on in the house, and it wasn't too long before my husband came and said this plantation owner said I would have to leave if I didn't go down and withdraw.

About that time, the man walked up, Mr. Marlow, and he said, "Is Fannie Lou back yet?"

My husband said, "She is."

I walked out of the house at this time. He said, "Fannie Lou, you have been to the courthouse to try to register," and he said, "We are not ready for this in Mississippi."

I said, "I didn't register for you, I tried to register for myself."

He said "We are not going to have this in Mississippi, and you will have to withdraw. I am looking for your answer, yea or nay."

I just looked. He said,"I will give you until tomorrow morning. And if you don't withdraw, you will have to leave." . . . So I left that same night.

On the 10th of September, they fired into the home of Mr. and Mrs. Robert Tucker 16 times for me. That same night, two girls were shot at Mr. Herman Sissel's. Also, they shot Mr. Joe Maglon's house. I was fired that day and haven't had a job since.

In 1963, I attended a voter registration workshop and was returning back to Mississippi. At Winona, Miss., I was arrested there. Some folk had got off the bus . . . to go into the restaurant to get food. Two of the people decided to use the restroom. I saw them come right straight out of the restaurant. I got off the bus to see what had happened. Miss Ponder said, "They won't let us eat." She said, "There was a chief of police and a highway patrolman inside, and they ordered us out." I said, "Well, this is Mississippi."

I got back on the bus, and about the time I just got sat down good, I looked out the window, and they were getting Miss Ponder and the others into the highway patrolman's car.

I stepped off the bus to see what was happening, and one screamed, "Get that one there." I was picked up, the police,

Earl Wane Patric (sic), told me I was under arrest. He opened the door, and as I started to get in, he kicked me. They carried me to town to this county jail.

We were carried to the booking room. Soon as we walked inside, I was in the car with Earl Wane Patric and one plain clothesman. I don't know whether he was a policeman or not. He didn't have on police clothes, had a crew haircut. They would ask me questions going on to jail, and as I would go on to answer, they would curse me and tell me to hush.

I was carried on to the booking room and carried from the booking room to a cell. After I was locked up in a cell with Miss Euvester Simpson, I began to hear the sounds of licks, and I could hear people screaming. I don't know how long it lasted before I saw Miss Ponder, the southside supervisor for SCLC [Southern Christian Leadership Conference], pass the cell with both her hands up. Her eyes looked like blood, and her mouth was swollen. She passed my cell. Her clothes was torn. She backed and they carried her again out of my sight.

After then, the State highway patrolman walked into my cell with two other white men. He asked where I was from, and I told him. He said, "I am going to check."

They left my cell, and it wasn't too long before they returned, and he said, "You damn right, you are from Ruleville," and he called me a bad name. He said they would make me wish I was dead.

I was carried out of the cell into another cell where there were two Negro prisoners. The State highway patrolman gave the first Negro a long blackjack that was heavy. It was loaded with something, and they had me lay down on the bunk with my face down, and I was beat, I was beat by the first Negro until I was exhausted.

After I was beaten by the first Negro, the State highway patrolman ordered the other Negro to take the blackjack. The second Negro, he began to beat. The State highway patrolman ordered the first Negro that had beat me to sit on my feet. One of the white men that was in the room, my dress would work up because it had a large skirt, but I was trying to keep it down and trying to shield the licks from the left side, because I had polio when I was a child. During the time that I was trying to work my dress down and keep the licks off my left side, one of the white men walked over and pulled my dress up.

At this time I had to hug around the mattress to keep the sound from coming out. . . .

Q. Mrs. Hamer, what was the charge on which you were arrested on the bus incident?

A. Well, . . . I asked the jailer, "Would you leave the door open so I could catch air." During the time the door was open, I heard discussion: "Now, what is we going to charge them with?" Somebody said something. He said, "Well, you are going to have to get up something better than that. Man, that is the end of the wire."

So I actually didn't know what we were charged with until they got ready to have our trial, and we were charged with resisting arrest and disorderly conduct. . . .

My husband was fired the day after I qualified to run as Congresswoman in the Second Congressional District. Last week he had gotten a second job. The mayor went out on this job on which he was working, so he will probably be fired by the time I get back home.

From *Congressional Record,* June 16, 1964.

Afterword

The revolution in race relations is taking place here and now. For a hundred years white Americans comfortably assured themselves that time alone would take care of the "race problem." But time by itself does nothing. It is people like Fannie Lou Hamer who make history. By taking their lives in their own hands and struggling to make them better, they have started a revolution. Down deepest in the social heap, they are ready to make the greatest change. Demonstrating in the streets, boycotting businesses and schools, organizing freedom schools, tenant leagues, cooperatives, and voter education projects, running candidates for office, the Negro has forced America to an awareness that basic social and economic changes are needed if there is to be a real equality among all citizens, black and white.

For in the many years since the Supreme Court's historic desegregation decision, it has become clear that the affirmation of basic democratic rights on paper is one thing; their realiza-

tion in Harlem or Watts or Selma is another. Schools, jobs, housing, civil rights—steps toward progress in these fields are being taken every day, but the pace is slow; the goals are still distant; the gaps between white and Negro in some areas are still as wide or even wider. Picket lines help, but they alone cannot solve the problems of slums, poor schools, bad housing, or unemployment.

Where poverty exists, the Negro gets more than his share of it. And why should anyone, black or white—in so rich and powerful a nation— have to live in poverty? The Negro revolution has made America think about these questions, and seek for answers.

A CALENDAR
OF NEGRO HISTORY

1917–1966

1917 America enters World War I. Race riots in East St. Louis, Illinois, and Houston, Texas. 10,000 Negroes march in silent protest parade down Fifth Avenue, New York City.

1918 Race riots in Chester, and Philadelphia, Pennsylvania. World War I ends: 370,000 Negro troops and 1,400 officers served, about half of them overseas in Europe. First U.S. Army men to be decorated for bravery in France are the Negroes Henry Johnson and Needham Roberts. Three Negro regiments receive Croix de Guerre for valor.

1919 W. E. B. DuBois organizes First Pan-African Congress in Paris. In "Red Summer" of 1919, 26 race riots take place.

1920 10,463,131 Negroes in United States, 9.9 per cent of population. Black nationalist movement headed by Marcus Garvey wins mass following.

1921 Race riot in Tulsa, Oklahoma. Negro Renaissance in the arts begins. Claude McKay, Jean Toomer, Alain Locke, W. C. Handy, Langston Hughes, Charles Gilpin, Paul Robeson, Countee Cullen, Rudolph Fisher, Wallace Thurman, James Weldon Johnson, Fletcher Henderson, King Oliver, Florence Mills, Noble Sissle, Eubie Blake, Duke Ellington, Louis Armstrong—poets, novelists, musicians, actors—make many contributions in the twenties.

1922 Carter Woodson's *The Negro in Our History* appears.

1923 Charles S. Johnson launches *Opportunity: Journal of Negro Life*.

1924 *Crisis* and *Opportunity* begin offering prizes to encourage creativity.

1927 Supreme Court rules unconstitutional a Texas law barring Negroes from voting in Democratic primary elections (*Nixon vs. Herndon*). Charles Wesley publishes *Negro Labor in the United States*.

1928 Franz Boas, Columbia University anthropologist, begins scientific attack on racist theories with his book, *Anthropology and Modern Life*.

1929 New York stock market collapses and Great Depression begins. Oscar de Priest, Chicago Republican, is first Negro to go to Congress since 1901.

1930 11,891,143 Negroes in United States, 9.7 per cent of population.

1931 Trial of nine Negro youths begins at Scottsboro, Alabama. Charged with raping two white women on a freight train, the "Scottsboro Boys" become an international *cause célèbre. The Journal of Negro Education* founded.

1933 Franklin D. Roosevelt takes office after winning presidency in Democratic landslide. His "New Deal" tries to combat depression, which hits Negroes hardest, by putting through many emergency measures and projects. NAACP begins attack on segregation and discrimination in education through legal suits.

1934 De Priest is replaced in Congress, losing to a Negro Democrat, Arthur L. Mitchell.

1935 American Negroes protest Italy's invasion of Ethiopia. Race riot in Harlem. National Council of Negro Women formed in New York.

1936 Jesse Owens wins four gold medals at Berlin Olympics. NAACP files first suit to eliminate pay differentials between Negro and white teachers. Mary McLeod Bethune is made director of Division of Negro Affairs of National Youth Administration.

1937 Joe Louis wins heavyweight championship from James J. Braddock. William H. Hastie appointed first Negro federal judge.

1938 Supreme Court rules that a state must provide equal educational facilities for Negroes within the state. Crystal Bird Fauset of Philadelphia, elected a state Representative, becomes first Negro woman legislator.

1939 Jane M. Bolin, appointed judge of New York City's Court of Domestic Relations, becomes first Negro woman judge in U.S. E. Franklin Frazier publishes *The Negro Family in the United States.*

1940 12,865,518 Negroes in United States, 9.8 per cent of population. Richard Wright publishes *Native Son*. *Phylon* founded in Atlanta with W. E. B. DuBois as editor. Benjamin O. Davis appointed brigadier general, first Negro to become general in U.S. armed forces.

1941 First Army Air Corps squadron for Negro cadets formed by War Department at Tuskegee. New York bus companies agree to hire Negro drivers and mechanics. March on Washington Movement wins from President Roosevelt his Executive Order 8802, forbidding racial and religious discrimination in war plants, government training programs, and government industries. Fair Employment Practices Commission is appointed to carry out order. Supreme Court rules separate facilities on railroads must be equal. Dorie Miller of Texas earns Navy Cross for downing four Japanese planes in attack on Pearl Harbor.

1942 Race riot in Detroit, one of several racial incidents to occur during war. U.S. Navy gives first commission to a Negro, Harvard medical student Bernard W. Robinson. Congress of Racial Equality organized in Chicago and stages first sit-in in local restaurant. Hugh Mulzac is first Negro captain to command a U.S. merchant ship, the *Booker T. Washington*.

1943 Race riots in Mobile, Beaumont, Detroit, Harlem. Paul Robeson stars in *Othello* and Anne Brown and Todd Duncan in *Porgy and Bess*.

1944 Supreme Court rules Negro cannot be denied right to vote in a primary election (Smith *vs.* Allwright). Adam Clayton Powell of New York is first Negro Congressman to be elected in the East.

1945 New York is first state to adopt an FEPC law. World War II ends with 1,154,720 Negroes having served in the armed forces.

1946 Race riots in Tennessee, Alabama, and Philadelphia. William H. Hastie appointed governor of the Virgin Islands. Supreme Court bans segregation in interstate bus travel. President Truman issues Executive Order establishing Committee on Civil Rights.

1947 First Freedom Rider group sent by CORE on Southern tour. Jackie Robinson of Brooklyn Dodgers is first Negro to play in big league baseball. "To Secure These Rights," report attacking racial injustice in U.S., is issued by President's Commission on Civil Rights. NAACP appeals to the United Nations on same issue.

1948 Supreme Court rules that a state must provide legal education for Negroes at the same time it provides it for whites, and that federal and state courts may not enforce restrictive covenants in housing. President Truman issues executive order requiring equality of treatment and opportunity in the armed forces.

1949 William Hastie is nominated for U.S. Circuit Court of Appeals. William L. Dawson, chosen chairman of House Expenditures Committee, is first Negro to head standing committee of Congress. Wesley A. Brown is first Negro graduated from Annapolis Naval Academy.

1950 15,042,286 Negroes in United States, 10 per cent of population. Ralph J. Bunche wins Nobel Prize for peace and Gwendolyn Brooks wins Pulitzer Prize for poetry. Supreme Court rules that equality in education involves more than physical facilities, rules that students admitted to a school cannot be segregated, and bans Jim Crow in railroad dining cars.

1951 Racial segregation is ruled illegal in restaurants of Washington, D.C., and racial discrimination is prohibited in New York's city-assisted housing projects. The first Negro student is admitted to the University of North Carolina. An NAACP official in Florida, Harry T. Moore, is killed when his home is wrecked by a bomb.

1952 This is the first year since 1881 for which the Tuskegee Institute record shows no lynchings in the U.S.

1953 Whites begin protracted series of riots to protest against Negroes moving into Chicago's Trumbull Park housing project. Rufus Clement elected to Atlanta Board of Education and Hulan Jack to borough presidency of Manhattan. President Eisenhower sets up Government Contract Compliance Committee to police ban on antidiscrimination in government contracts.

1954 Supreme Court rules that racial segregation in public schools is unconstitutional. School integration begins in the capital and in Baltimore. Negro units are abolished in the armed forces. Dr. Peter M. Marshall becomes president of New York County Medical Society, first AMA unit with a Negro leader. Charles C. Diggs, Jr. is elected Michigan's first Negro Congressman. Benjamin O. Davis, Jr. appointed first Negro general in Air Force.

1955 Supreme Court orders school integration "with all deliberate speed," and bans segregation in public recreation facilities. Segregation in buses, waiting rooms, and railroad coaches in interstate travel is banned by Interstate Commerce Commission. Marian Anderson is first Negro to sing in Metropolitan Opera. Emmet Till, 14, is kidnapped and lynched in Mississippi. Bus boycott begins in Montgomery, Alabama, under leadership of Rev. Martin Luther King, Jr.

1956 Autherine J. Lucy admitted to University of Alabama but expelled 26 days later. Supreme Court upholds ban on segregation in intrastate bus travel. Bus boycotts in Birmingham and Tallahassee. National Guard used to quell mobs trying to prevent school integration in Clinton, Tennessee, and Sturgis, Kentucky. Louisville integrates its public schools.

1957 Southern Christian Leadership Conference organized in New Orleans; Rev. Martin Luther King, Jr. elected president. First Civil Rights Act since 1875 passed by Congress. Federal troops ordered to Little Rock to ensure that nine Negro children enter Central High School. Tuskegee Negroes boycott merchants to protest gerrymander depriving Negroes of municipal vote. New York City's Fair Housing Practice Law is first municipal measure against racial and religious discrimination in housing.

1958 Sit-ins used to desegregate Oklahoma City lunch counters. Philadelphia elects Robert N. C. Nix to Congress. Clifton R. Wharton becomes Minister to Rumania.

1959 To prevent school integration Prince Edward County in Virginia closes public school system. First play written by Negro woman, Lorraine Hansberry's *Raisin in the Sun,* is hit on Broadway. Mack Parker lynched in Poplarville, Mississippi.

1960 18,871,831 Negroes in United States, 10.5 per cent of population. Students of North Carolina A. and T. College begin sit-in movement at five-and-ten store in Greensboro, North Carolina. Tactic swiftly adopted by students in 15 cities in five Southern states. First Southern city to integrate lunch counters is San Antonio. National chain stores follow in over 100 cities. Thousands of students arrested in demonstrations, some suspended by colleges. Student Nonviolent Coordinating Committee organized at Shaw University. Congress passes Civil Rights Act of 1960. Large demonstrations against Jim Crow in Atlanta.

1961 Adam Clayton Powell becomes chairman of House Education and Labor Committee. Robert Weaver made chief of Housing and Home Finance Agency, highest federal appointment thus far for a Negro. Otis M. Smith appointed to Michigan Supreme Court. Freedom Riders on bus trip through South attacked, bombed, burned, arrested in Alabama and Mississippi. ICC prohibits segregation on buses and in terminal facilities. President Kennedy appoints Thurgood Marshall to U.S. Circuit Court of Appeals. Militant Albany Movement uses mass marches on City Hall to protest segregation and discrimination in that Georgia city. Board of Education of New Rochelle, New York, ordered by judge to integrate schools.

1962 James H. Meredith, escorted by federal marshals, registered at University of Mississippi after 12,000 federal soldiers restore order on rioting campus. Two are killed and over 100 wounded in violence touched off at Governor Ross Barnett's defiance of federal court order to admit Meredith. SNCC works on voter registration in South, especially in Mississippi. Pressure applied against *de facto* segregation in Northern school systems. President Kennedy issues order against racial and religious discrimination in federally financed housing.

1963 Centennial of Emancipation Proclamation is celebrated by intensified campaigns for civil rights. Two Negro students enrolled at University of Alabama under escort of federal troops. Medgar Evers, NAACP leader in Mississippi, murdered in front of his home. Discrimination in building trades unions protested by mass demonstrations at Harlem building sites. A quarter of a million Negroes and whites take part in March on Washington for civil rights. Four Negro children killed when Birmingham church is bombed. 225,000 students boycott Chicago public schools for one day to protest *de facto* segregation.

1964 Almost a million students boycott New York City public schools on one day and another quarter million students on a later day. Civil Rights Act with public accommodation and fair employment sections passed by Congress and signed by President Lyndon B. Johnson on July 3 after Senate uses cloture to stop a Southern filibuster. Race riots erupt in New York City, Rochester, Jersey City, Chicago, Philadelphia. Civil rights organizations undertake Mississippi Freedom Project during summer, opening freedom schools and community centers and aiding Negroes to register to vote. Three young civil rights workers engaged in project are murdered by segregationists near Philadelphia, Mississippi. Freedom Democratic Party, organized in Mississippi, nominates three Negroes for Congress, the first since Reconstruction. Dr. Martin Luther King, Jr. is awarded the Nobel Prize for peace, viewing it as recognition of nonviolence precept.

1965 Negro voter registration drive launched in Selma, Alabama, by SCLC and SNCC. When violence is used against demonstrators on Selma bridge, a Selma-to-Montgomery march is held to dramatize Negro voting rights. 3,200 Negroes and whites from all over the nation go on march, protected by 4,000 troops. March ends with rally of 25,000 in front of the capitol in Montgomery. President Johnson signs the 1965 Voting Rights Act on August 7. Federal examiners begin to register Negroes under the Act, the first use of federal registrars since Reconstruction. The new act provides for suspension of literacy tests and for federal registration of Negroes in states and subdivisions where less than 50 per cent of the voting age population were registered or enrolled in November, 1964. The areas covered by the law include two million unregistered Negroes. Riots occur in the Watts area of Los Angeles and in Chicago. Negroes end a three-month boycott of white merchants in Natchez after the city government and business leaders agree to demands for a voice in city affairs.

1966 Dr. Robert C. Weaver, appointed Secretary of Housing and Urban Development, becomes first Negro Cabinet member. Constance Baker Motley is first Negro woman appointed a federal judge. U.S. Supreme Court rules Virginia poll tax unconstitutional, thereby ending tax in three other Southern states. Negro group occupies deactivated U.S. Air Force base in Greenville, Mississippi, protesting lack of jobs and land. James Meredith begins 200-mile march from Memphis to Jackson to bolster voting registration, and is shot in back from ambush. Other civil rights leaders join march, which concludes with rally of 15,000 before state capitol at Jackson. In Mississippi primaries, 35,000 Negroes vote, largest number in state in twentieth century. Slogan of "Black Power," raised by SNCC leader Stokely Carmichael during Mississippi march, becomes national issue. Rev. Martin Luther King, Jr., opens assault by SCLC on slum conditions in Chicago. Riots occur in several urban ghettoes, especially Chicago and Cleveland.

READING LIST

Bontemps, Arna, and Jack Conroy. *Anyplace But Here*. New York: Hill and Wang, 1966.
>A new revised edition of the history of Negro migration within the United States, including many biographical sketches.

Broderick, Francis L., and August Meier, editors. *Negro Protest Thought in the Twentieth Century*. Indianapolis: Bobbs-Merrill, 1966.
>A large collection of documents illustrating all the major points of view voiced by Negro leadership.

Davis, John P., editor. *The American Negro Reference Book*. Englewood Cliffs: Prentice-Hall, 1966.
>An extensive sourcebook of facts on almost every aspect of Negro life from colonial times to the present, compiled by 126 experts.

Franklin, John Hope. *From Slavery to Freedom*. New York: Knopf, 1956.
>The classic, most detailed, one-volume history of American Negroes, by one of the best authorities.

Hentoff, Nat. *The New Equality*. New York: Viking, 1965.
>An analysis of the Negro freedom movement of the 1960s.

Hughes, Langston, and Milton Meltzer. *A Pictorial History of the Negro in America*. New York: Crown, 1963.
>Over 1,000 prints, drawings, paintings, photos, broadsides, cartoons, posters are combined with a swift narrative in a panoramic history that comes down to the Freedom Movement of the 1960s.

Hughes, Langston, and Milton Meltzer. *Black Magic: A Pictorial History of the Negro in American Entertainment*. Englewood Cliffs: Prentice-Hall, 1967.
>A panoramic view of the Negro's contributions to American theatre, dance, music, radio, television, films, from slavery times to the present.

Lewis, Anthony, and *The New York Times*. *Portrait of a Decade*. New York: Bantam Books, 1965.
>A vivid chronicle of the years 1954-1965, with many excerpts from articles and news reports in *The New York Times* and useful charts and maps.

Logan, Rayford W. *The Negro in the United States*. Princeton: D. Van Nostrand, 1957.
>A short history combined with several key documents.

Meltzer, Milton, and August Meier. *Time of Trial, Time of Hope: The American Negro 1919-1941*. New York: Zenith Books, Doubleday, 1966.
>A brief, illustrated account of two crucial decades, stressing the migration North, the artistic renaissance of the twenties, the Great Depression and the New Deal.

Quarles, Benjamin. *The Negro in the Making of America*. New York: Collier Books, 1964.
>A very readable survey of the Negro's past that does more than present him as a "problem"—it shows his positive contributions to American life.

Warren, Robert Penn. *Who Speaks for the Negro?* New York: Vintage Books, 1966.
>Tape-recorded interviews with Negroes from every part of the nation who are making the civil rights revolution.

Zinn, Howard. *SNCC: The New Abolitionists*. Boston: Beacon Press, 1964.
>A first-hand account of the Student Nonviolent Coordinating Committee by a historian and teacher who was one of SNCC's advisors.

INDEX

INDEX